W9-BHT-805

Acknowledgements

Our work here has been the result of the dedicated enthusiasm of many people, especially those who frequently read our manuscript. So as not to praise the blame worthy nor blame the praise worthy, as the Greek Sophist, Gorgias, argued, we wish to thank all those who supported in word and deed the writing of our work.

They include our wives, Susan and Janie, and our children, Lisa, John, and David G (also responsible for the design of the book's cover), Jason, and David M. They enthusiastically embraced our project, never complaining, always suggesting. The love and support of our families sustained us through the four years we needed to finish this work.

Other readers whose advice proved invaluable were neighbors and colleagues: Steven and Susan Wolfson, Graham Gibbard, Sheryll Bedingfield, Anna Follis, Marie Furmanski, Amy Evangelisto and Martin Spear.

Mike Guidice rendered the drawings of Janis and Jim in therapy as well as in the beginning of the first chapter.

We alone are responsible for any and all errors.

Special thanks to Crown Publishers for permission to cite from Buried Alive by Myra Friedman. Copyright @ 1992 by Myra Friedman. Reprinted by permission of Crown Publishers, Inc.

Foreword

The Connecticut Turnpike stretched well ahead of us on that warm spring day as my brother and I drove to a family reunion in Massachusetts. It would be another two and half hours before we would arrive at my cousin's impressive home, a former convent that is now the headquarters for all important Faris family gatherings. I reached for the radio dial, hoping to find some relief from the broken white lines that marked the turnpike lanes, when a voice cried out, singing a melody that instantly carried us back to the 1960's, to the anti-war sentiments that filled the airways, to the epic struggle for civil rights, to the generation of flower children and the music they embraced so passionately. Janis Joplin was singing, and our journey was made ever so much more enjoyable, filled as it was with the memories that "Me and Bobby McGee" so quickly renewed.

As it turned out, we had unknowingly discovered a "golden oldie" station, so our two hundred mile journey led to inevitable reminiscing, to the tales we tell each other about what happened in our lives when Lyndon Johnson and Richard Nixon were president, when baseball's Mets were finally top dogs, and Vietnam was our major concern. We reminded each other how awful were the clothes that we once wore and the conflicts we had; but the music, oh that music, how intoxicating it was. All that from a song recorded almost twenty-five years ago.

As the music ended, we both remarked how young Janis was when she died, how her death was followed by that of Jim Morrison, also in the prime of his life. I let my mind wander back to the 1960s and deaths of two very talented performers whose music helped me to survive while leading a platoon of soldiers through the jungles of Vietnam.

Aware that I was emotionally surfing the sixties, my brother, speaking casually but knowledgeably about their deaths, said "They were tragic figures, struggling with a borderline condition, ya know," he calmly offered. "I've seen dozens just like them." "Borderline?" I asked, "What do you mean, borderline?" He was referring to borderline personality disorders, to highly neurotic and tormented people whose affliction is now very well documented in clinical literature. I was rather surprised by his confident voice, and asked him to explain why he was so certain that Janis and Jim were borderline personalities. For the next hour he offered me the insights he had gained through intense exchanges with his "borderline" patients, from the wealth of research and clinical case studies, and from the information about Janis and Jim discovered in their excellent biographies and other books detailing their everyday behaviors.

So that was it, I thought. Two masterful, charismatic but deeply disturbed artists died because at the time the basis for their tormented and self-destructive behaviors was not known; no one could help them because there was no help—not unlike the people who at one time died of pneumonia because there were no antibiotics. Worse still. My brother remarked that there are many, many undiagnosed borderline personalities who will remain so because many clinicians, even now, aren't adequately trained to identify such a disorder. And many people are misdiagnosed as borderline disorders because many clinicians are poorly trained to understand the difference between borderline disorders and other disorders, such as manic-depressive disorder, major depressive disorders and childhood based post traumatic stress disorder. He suggested that a more compelling kind of story might be useful in alerting therapists to symptoms that have been associated with the disorder. And that might just help to identify and treat patients who suffer from the same disorder that eventually killed Janis and Jim.

Acting on that conversation, my brother and I initially considered developing a "manual" of sorts that might be useful to therapists and clinicians. Later, however, as our interest in Janis and Jim intensified, we found ourselves entranced by the circumstances of their lives and by the dramatically oppositional and unpredictably volatile nature of the borderline disorder that afflicted them. We decided to dedicate our book to a wider, more popular audience—the one that loved and appreciated their music when they were alive, and those who still find a deep connection with their music almost thirty years after their deaths.

After all, we thought, shouldn't their fans, who were and are thrilled by their performances but saddened and mystified by their early, tragic deaths be offered insight into the inner core that powered their compelling and often haunting lyrics and music? Convinced of their fans' enduring interest, we constructed this post-1960s social-psychological analysis of Janis Joplin and Jim Morrison.

Preface

No two people captured the imagination and emotions of the "sixties" generation as did Janis Joplin and Jim Morrison. Their dramatic stories have been told in numerous biographies, in film, and in their music. They entered a social arena during a decade characterized by radical social movements, widespread rebellion, and popular unrest. The distant but deadly southeast Asian war and the historic struggle of civil rights groups afforded Janis and Jim the opportunity to generate extraordinary psychedelic sonatas aimed directly at the dissatisfied, the alienated, and the young. Their early deaths increased the passion felt by their fans, spurred numerous films, internet web pages and biographies. Their characters and deaths also guaranteed a consistently high demand for their music, now technologically enhanced, which endures even among those too young to have experienced the tumult of the sixties.

Thus, more than twenty-five years after their tragic deaths a persistent fascination with their lives remains intact. New biographies exploring the life and times of Janis and Jim were published in 1990, 1991, 1992 and 1993. New releases of their recordings are planned or are already released. Films of their concerts and interviews are stocked in video stores. Younger generations of Americans are intrigued by the music of Janis and Jim if not by the aura surrounding their deaths. *Newsweek* (7/15/93) reported that during the first six months of 1993 more than 500,000 Door records and over 200,000 Joplin albums were sold.

Conversations about Janis and Jim evoke positive and highly emotional responses. One young sales clerk told us she absolutely loved and adored Jim Morrison while wrinkling her nose at Janis Joplin. Another, noticing that we were purchasing a Joplin tape, volunteered exuberantly, "She's great, she's super." and asked us if we had read Myra Friedman's *Buried Alive.* People in their forties who remember Janis and Jim and who may have also seen them in concert recall them as incredible, wild, unbelievable, and then usually add approvingly, "crazy." Those under thirty think of the two as fantastic and legendary free spirits whose lives ended tragically.

Why then this book? A number of excellent biographies on Janis and Jim have been published. Filmed interviews and documentaries are readily available in video stores along with their music. Their lives have been captured in motion pictures (Janis in a story called *The Rose* and Jim in Oliver Stone's *The Doors*). What new light, then, can we shed on their lives?

All the publicly available information on Janis and Jim is *descriptive,* that is, it describes their behavior, temperament, moods and personalities, and records faithfully the course of their lives and careers. What that information doesn't provide is a reasonable explanation for the dissonant and relentlessly self-destructive behavior that led to their premature deaths. Serious biographers have been compassionate and psychologically perceptive in describing the desperation and torment of each, but have exhibited little interest in or ability to identify the underlying causes of their disorders. And that is not surprising.

Determining causality is understandably complicated and risky when done from a distance. This has not prevented some from engaging in such risky business, however. Popular explanatory accounts of the lives of Janis and Jim tend to disclose more about how little the authors know about the dynamics of psychological disorders than they do about Janis and Jim. These surface level analyses have typically pointed to their abuse of alcohol and drugs as if that were a sufficient explanation by itself. Others blame self-destructive patterns of depression rooted in early family conflicts, traumatic incidents in their lives, or the overwhelming pressures created by fame and stardom. But, as we hope to reveal, the root causes of the extended and debilitating despair suffered by these two tragic talents has simply not been established.

This book has come about by chance. We had planned originally to explore the lives of several famous people (Joplin, Morrison, Monroe, Hendrix, Garland and others) for the purpose of uncovering the forces responsible for their widely publicized distress. In addition to these "stars," we also intended to examine certain characters from literature and movies. As our research progressed, we became increasingly fascinated with the accounts of the lives of Janis and Jim, experiencing a deep sense of sadness at what we learned about their greatly troubled existence. In Janis' case, we were struck by what appeared to be a deeply felt pain she exhibited in news clips which captured her unrelenting hopelessness. In those clips, she behaves as a child who is alternately angry, charming, confused, and witty while answering questions from reporters. We read of her search for love in an attempt to quiet the internal demons through endless, transient sexual liaisons, and her wild partying and alcohol abuse. Like Janis, Jim struggled unsuccessfully for meaning by avoiding or running from a similar feeling of hopelessness. Thus his life too was characterized by aggressive behaviors, alcoholism, and antics for which he was so well known.

Both are and were presented in public and in private as highly neurotic and disordered, and as lacking the resources which we all need to soothe ourselves when alone: the ability to make our existence tolerable, to experience satisfaction from relationships, and to possess a sense of ourselves and our continuity. It is this deficit, this missing quality of their inner world, that was at the root of the persistent and debilitating hopelessness they both experienced. That hopelessness is what faces those unfortunate enough to find themselves living in the dead zone—a term frequently used by my patients to describe how their *borderline personality disorder* feels to them (described in detail in the first chapter).

Prologue

I know Janis Joplin. She's been in my office many times. I have seen her funky clothes, heard her cackling laugh, been the target of her good-natured wisecracks, experienced her unpredictable *affect* storms, and felt her agony. I have lamented the dismal, pitiable quality of her life, wrestled with her demons, and tried to help her with the most intractable of inner conflicts. And I've observed her relentless drive toward self-destruction.

Jim Morrison, too, has been in my office. Like Janis, he was bleeding from self-inflicted wounds. Unlike Janis, though, his demeanor was frequently abstruse and enigmatic, his ever present arrogance being the most prominent feature of his interactions with others. He uses words to confuse, attack, and diffuse, yet his demons, like Janis', were unmerciful and, in the end, do not permit him to escape. Finally he fell victim to them as he slid into the abyss.

I have seen patients in my office who bear a close psychological resemblance to Janis and Jim. I know them from my experiences with patients in psychiatric hospitals, with patients in my private practice, and with patients of interns and clinicians I have supervised. Of course, my patients are not exactly like Janis or Jim. No person is ever identical to another—not even identical twins. People have their own unique combination of traits apart from their pathology, as do my patients. But they are very similar to Janis and Jim in that they engage in the same terrible struggle with the emptiness of the dead zone.

Overcome by constant misery and beset by a vast and dreadful emotional emptiness, they were unable to contain the forces that drive their rampant impulsivity. Lacking a stable sense of self and vulnerable to sudden emotional episodes, they desperately seek to sustain unsustainable relationships, as did Janis and Jim. Like my patients, they led lives that were both intense and chaotic.

One should not, however, misconstrue the analysis we

provide in this book as an attempt to diminish the value of their creativity or of their contributions as performing artists. Nor should one take this work to be yet another exposé of the "real" lives of two rock stars. Janis and Jim should not and cannot be *defined* solely by their affliction, and it is certainly true that their lives, regrettably, have been greatly exploited.

Still, we do wonder how they were able to bring so much energy, creativity and excitement to their music in spite of "living in the dead zone." Speculating in that direction might be intriguing, but it is an activity nonetheless that will hardly produce a useful response. Instead, we attempt to understand the psychological roots of their illnesses, which eventually ended in tragedy. We provide explanations of their behavior which are drawn from more recent developments in modern psychiatry and psychology—developments that we think involve the most comprehensive account of the disorder that ultimately took their lives.

[GAF]

Jim

There are twenty cemeteries in Paris. In one, Pere LaChaise, are the graves of Chopin, Sarah Bernhardt, Oscar Wilde, Marcel Proust, Gertrude Stein, Isadora Duncan, and Balzac. And Jim Morrison.

The weather was overcast and cool during a visit to Paris in the fall of 1993 when I (GAF) spent a few hours at the cemetery researching this book. The ubiquitous French penchant for decoration and style can be seen at Pere LaChaise, in the well kept, sometimes elaborately designed grave sites, many with small altars inside a larger stone chamber above the ground. On ordinary days, the cemetery is filled with people visiting loved ones. Uncharacteristically, many of the visitors were young, ranging in age from fourteen to twenty-three or twenty-four. They came in large numbers, guided by the notorious but revealing graffiti on the monuments leading to Jim Morrison's grave. All of them, like the weather that day, were somber and solemn, tombstone tourists trekking in seemingly endless numbers, and seemingly hoping for some kind of emotional experience at the grave of a man who was dead before they were born.

Uniformed guards have been permanently stationed at Jim Morrison's grave for the past twenty or so years to prevent it from being destroyed piecemeal by visitors. The damage to other gravesites has been so extensive that the French may refuse to renew the lease for Jim's plot (Jim's gravesite at Pere LaChaise was leased not purchased). Everywhere along the way, the graffiti spray painted on other grave sites reflects the intense feelings that Morrison could elicit. The diverse, often contradictory messages expressed in the graffiti are fascinating. Read perspicaciously, they underscore how his music was interpreted by his fans, by those to whom he expressed his hopes and conflicts, and often his rather dark assessment of life's possibilities. There were many of the symbols from the peace movement of the sixties and "I love you Jim" with a signature. Others wrote the name or lyrics of some of his songs like "The end my friend," and "Break on Through," as if they were by themselves prophetic. A few with troubled minds wrote things like "Kill parents."

Many Morrison fans appear reflective, sad, gloomy and/or nettlesome, more like Morrison himself, absorbed with existential matters, sex, and death. Much of Morrison's music amplified such concerns, as in "The End," "Five To One," "When the Music's Over," and "Unknown Soldier." Odd and mystifying feelings are expressed in such songs as "People are Strange," "Strange Days," and "I Can't See Your Face In My Mind". He characteristically acted in weird, obnoxious ways on stage—actions that seemed to have had no purpose other than to allow him to dissipate pent up tensions.

I interviewed dozens of these young mourners from Germany, France, Belgium, England, Italy, Austria, and the United States. Without exception, in their mood and manner they revealed a reverence for, and a strong identification with, Jim Morrison. These young people derived whatever meaning they needed from the music, poetry, and antics of Jim Morrison's life in order to cope with the conflicts and deep tensions of their own adolescent struggles. Their misreadings of Morrison varied. Some thought of him as a free spirit, others as a rebel with a cause. They knew of his self-destructive behavior but chose to disregard it. He was their hero, no qualifications necessary.

Janis

Janis Joplin is not buried anywhere. In *Buried Alive* Myra Friedman writes that Janis's body was cremated in accordance with her will and her ashes scattered by air along the coastline of Marin County, California. Thus no pilgrimage to a Janis Joplin shrine is possible. Fans have to make do with her music, a documentary film called Janis, and a bronze statue of her in several of her well known stage postures located in the Port Arthur Historical Collection at the Lamar University Library in Port Arthur, Texas. Her fans, however, are no less dedicated.

Ask anyone who attended a Joplin concert and in a flash of

memory he or she will return to the scene. One fifty year-old Ph.D. who had seen Janis in concert told me, "It was extraordinary. She had gotten a hold on the deepest passions of the audience. It was an incredible scene. Constant motion, erupting like a volcano, holding nothing back—you had to be there. I'll never forget it."

If you talk to enough fans of the two great singers, you will quickly hear the noticeable difference in the kind of responses elicited from fans of Janis as opposed to Jim's. Though Joplin fans, like Morrison's, make of her what they need, and see her as sympathetic to the conflicts they feel, what most distinguishes them is what, after all distinguished Jim from Janis: different psychological agendas.

Janis' fans give off a softer feeling of exuberance and a "go for the fun of it" attitude. They talk of Janis as a life-loving, good-time girl who wasn't going to be bound by "dumb" rules, and as one who spoke her mind. Like Janis, her fans are preoccupied with matters of life, hope, love, and sex. One can easily discern these preoccupations in songs such as "Try," "One Good Man," "Piece of My Heart," and, in general, from her public persona of "Get It While You Can." Thus, it's not stretching the truth to suggest her fans embraced those themes.

The two are alive and well, then. Their songs, antics, and agony are remembered well by the many who *felt* the conflicts to which Janis and Jim referred. Increasingly new CD's and tapes can be found on the shelves of music stores as their music is recycled and updated year after year. Each of these performers possessed a unique quality of style and content, of personality and intensity that appeals to similar audiences. That the music of two deceased rock stars has such a following is not unusual. However, such psychological and emotional elements of the Morrison and Joplin phenomenon are seldom found and rarely to the extent we observe today. Even the enthusiasm popularly expressed for Elvis Presley's music has more to do with the nostalgic response of the generation which actually heard the music than it does with deep feelings of emptiness and despair. The Joplin and Morrison phenomenon arises from the more primitive, conflicted elements of psychological development and thus has the potential to reach an audience that cuts across generations.

We believe there is great irony in the fans' perception of these two stars because much of their behavior was misinterpreted. Fans were encouraged and comforted by Janis and Jim's excesses, their search for thrills, their intense, rowdy, impatient, attention-seeking, chaotic behavior. In actuality these self-destructive tendencies were symptomatic of something more. Little did fans know that Janis and Jim were two unique, eccentric but talented people experiencing the unrelenting, existential despair that is characteristically found in certain personality types—personalities who were destined to live their lives in a constant struggle with the hopelessness of life in the *dead zone*.

Chapter One: Living in the Dead Zone

A mind is not to be changed by place or time.
The mind is its own place, and in itself
Can make a heav'n of hell, a hell of heav'n.

Milton : Paradise Lost

Since the deaths of Janis and Jim, psychologists have developed many promising explanations, complete with technical terms, of that awful place the mind harbors. So if you consult the appropriate journals you will encounter terms such as "object inconstancy," "object impermanence," "identity disturbance," and "splitting," to name a few. Each term has been used to describe some feature of the environment that patients refer to as the dead zone. All the terms taken together are supposed to offer a complete picture of that experience. But these terms, so carefully developed by clinical researchers, simply do not grasp the terrible psychological toll paid by people who experience the emptiness of that zone. Widely heralded icons of music, Janis and Jim never really knew what the zone was, though they were driven into that dark and foreboding place most of their adult lives.

Imagine a mind teetering on the edge of an unimaginable abyss, a devastating emptiness in which there is no self, no other, and no reference points—a terrifying nothingness, a null point of mind. While encompassed in the nothingness, the mind experiences a confounding chaos of confusing noise and an indescribable sense of catastrophe. Unable to grasp or comprehend the reality of others, the mind thus cannot comprehend itself. The totality of the experience leaves the sufferer with no "I" feelings, no sense of actually existing, no self-reality. The continuity of self-feelings, moment to moment, is relentlessly broken by the emptiness, the spacelessness, the nothingness.

Imagine next the frantic scrambling for a person or place to provide an unchanging, reliable anchor, a reassuring "rock of Gibraltar" to quiet the noise and fill in the spacelessness so that the mind might perceive its own existence. The mind's hope is to achieve but a modicum of the necessary "I" feeling, of a convincing reality of one's self. A struggle ensues, a battle begins.

Janis and Jim died because they could not comprehend that the hell they made for themselves came from their own minds. A little understood disorder in the 1960s, their affliction engulfed, them leaving no way out, no relief. One of the most complicated and disruptive states of being, it is difficult for someone in it to describe and almost impossible for those not there to imagine. But it has been studied, identified and is now able to be treated with modest success. In clinical practice, it is currently known as *the borderline syndrome* or *borderline personality disorder.*

How can we describe Janis and Jim's condition? How can we make their experience of life in the dead zone comprehensible? They experienced one of the most complex and confusing disorders known in clinical psychology, then and now. What do we know about the disorder today that we didn't know when they were alive?

Perhaps we should start with the term most frequently used by patients in therapy to describe that state of mind, that place to which they are driven daily: the dead zone. Even if we had been able to interview Janis and Jim, we would have had great difficulty in obtaining unambiguous and revealing accounts of their tortuous, emotional experiences. And both were widely know to be very bright, articulate personalities. Nonetheless, we offer you a glimpse of that terrible place by tapping into the accounts offered by patients who have been thrust into the dead zone. Our book's title actually came from a patient who wrote that she was:

> . . . always scared and empty,
> like a void. Always feeling on
> edge. Will I always be like . .
> .this? I feel so all alone. No
> matter what, it's like I'm unreal,
> not here, like the living dead;
> no, not even dead . . . just . . .

nothing.

As is often the case with complex personality disorders, other patients not only offered different descriptive accounts, but rejected the qualifier "dead" for "zone," preferring instead terms such as intense conflict, or "non-zone." Another patient found different metaphors more helpful as she rejected the dead zone imagery altogether:

> It is not a zone, because to me
> that implies a place in which
> something is, an inexplicable
> oneness of being and peace. I
> am both the thing and the space
> and the time, and nothing comes
> in or out because there is no out
> or time or separateness . . . .

The snow metaphor seems more apt, it is a *whiteout*.

And, as if to emphasize her objection to the term *dead*, she added:

> I wish it were the dead zone
> because in such a place one
> could be free of feeling—for
> that is to me what dead
> implies—but it is a place void
> of understanding while full of
> feeling all the more painful
> feeling, because it is not capable
> of dying or ending or stopping
> or being understood by self or
> others. But to call it a dead zone
> is to misidentify it as well as
> those who inhabit it.

However differently patients may describe their borderline experiences, they experience, as did Janis and Jim, an inner world of feeling that leads to contradictions in their behavior, distorting and frequently destroying their perspective, their relations with others and their sense of well-being. Within them emotional tidal waves known as *affect storms* may rage for hours or days, reappearing and then suddenly disappearing, leaving their most valued friends exhausted, confused, and frustrated.

Because they were unable to control their emotional states for very long, they were to be controlled by them. Their behaviors consistently reflected this rule-by-chaos phenomenon. Researcher/clinician Marsha Linehan has suggested that people with this disorder "are like people with third degree burns over 90% of their bodies. Lacking emotional skin, they feel agony at the slightest touch or movement."

In *I Hate you—Don't Leave Me*, Kreisman and Straus describe the borderline disorder, as "emotional hemophilia; [a borderline patient] lacks the clotting mechanism needed to moderate his spurts of feeling. Stimulate a passion and the borderline emotionally bleeds to death."

That chaotic internal state of mind that characterized the lives of Janis and Jim was relentless and insidious. That they managed under those conditions to produce exciting and cutting edge music is remarkable; that they both died at a the top of their careers and at a very early age is, however, not surprising. They couldn't have realized that their overwhelming sense of desolation was not a widely shared experience. Janis and Jim dragged themselves through life while tormented by chronic feelings of emptiness, intense loneliness, blankness, and numbness, as if living in a black hole, constantly leaving them on the edge of confusion, wracked by intolerable tension, consumed by alienation and desolation. Generally, borderline patients usually do what Janis and Jim did, that is, create chaos and disorder, anger and despair where ever they go, including anyone who might be in their company.

So how can we distinguish the borderline from others? Like others living in the dead zone, Janis and Jim engaged in behaviors that destroyed many of their interpersonal relations. They shifted quickly from one emotional state to another, continually instigated self-damaging, impulsive actions, and in the process experienced profound and consuming identity conflicts. When asked, Janis and Jim would attempt to justify themselves with a long list of pseudo-rationalizations such as "I was angry, I'm being mistreated, I want to get it on man, get down, get groovin, I am incensed at injustice, I am just a rebel, I want to live life to the fullest, I was feeling bored, I'm just different and the world can't handle it," and so on, as if these explanations were entirely acceptable excuses for their aberrant behaviors.

The question we raise and answer in this book is whether Janis and Jim, with the help of a therapist, might have been able to assess their mental state more carefully. Might they have come to understand the inner world of feelings, comprehend the emptiness and dread of their own dead zones? Would they have begun to speak as others have of the dead zone as a *void*, a *nothingness*, a *state of not being*. Might they have been helped? We think so.

As clinicians have come to expect from borderline patients today, Janis and Jim continually felt listless, frequently complaining about mistreatment by others. They were often on the edge of agitation.

The tragedy is that they could not possibly have won the battle they waged against the disorder, not at that time. Psychology was not yet in a position to offer them relief, so misunderstood was their affliction.

Each seemed to have the problem dead zoners have: feeling "out of it", having to "rewrite" one's history to make sense of one's behavior, because each desperately needed reality to conform to what they were feeling in the moment. So personal history or incidents in their past were illegitimately interpreted to validate the present. The instability of their own "I" feeling impelled them to seek reassurance of their own existence. Jim Morrison relied on Pamela Courson to reestablish his "I" sense. Janis seemed to rely on letters to her family, her audiences, and a number of relationships which could not survive her self-destructive behavior. Both of them relied on alcohol and heroin

6

to blunt the despair of living in the dead zone.

Janis and Jim, like others in the zone, always appeared to be depressed, though without the longing, the sense of loss and grief characteristic of those who are clinically depressed. What depression they felt, if they felt anything, was merely secondary. Depressed people often have difficulty with appetite, sleep, concentration, and being interested in life, while people in the dead zone usually do not (unless they are clinically depressed in addition to being in the dead zone, suggesting multiple diagnoses). Janis and Jim had no identifiable loss or incident to account for any depressed mood and, from all the sources available on their lives, no family history of depression.

The following are three central characteristics that clinicians associate with the lives of people living in the dead zone.

1. Intense and chaotic efforts to escape the experience of the dead zone.

Like others suffering from this malady, Janis and Jim tended to create turbulence in their environment, and to act out in various ways by blocking, diffusing, masking or weakening the horrific, emptiness of the dead zone. Unaware of the root causes of their deep anxiety, they often behaved in ways typical of those trying to escape or contain the experience of these feelings. They frequently abused alcohol and drugs, engaged in sexual promiscuity, and behaved in emotionally unstable, dramatic or bizarre ways, to include explosive outbursts. Janis and Jim exhibited many of the personality **traits** found in varying combinations among people in need of escaping from the dead zone. Often both Janis and Jim could be:

chaotic	childish
cranky	hostile
moody	reckless
seductive	volatile
demanding	extreme
unreasonable	unpredictable
mercurial	intense.

The King and Queen of Rock and Roll also displayed some

of the following behaviors and symptoms:

outbursts of rage	diffuse anger or
chronic tension or anxiety	irritability
	panic attacks and acute
	anxiety
phobias	superficiality
moodiness	detachment
thrill-seeking	sexual escapades
emotional lability or	
emotional blandness	feelings of despair
physical complaints	clinging
anorexia	bulimia
alcohol or drug abuse	withdrawal
inappropriate gestures	emotional detachment
	cognitive and
	perceptual
distortions	suicidal ideation or
	dissociative experiences

Unaware of their affliction, both Janis and Jim engaged in these behaviors in their futile struggle to escape life in the dead zone.

2. A disturbance in identity formation or sense of self due to the dead zone.

The process of **identity formation** is complex. All humans must work through it. The lifelong, chaotic, and pervasive nature of that process in Janis and Jim suggested that condition to us. Janis and Jim, like many borderline patients, had loosely configured selves which were maintained through a career identity, while outside that career their cohesive self-feeling gradually dissolves. In both cases, they found people who become stabilizing figures (husband, wife, boss, parent, friend, mentor, etc.), people who periodically helped them maintain psychic balance. Jim Morrison had Pamela Courson while Janis apparently had several people over the years, and her family via letters from home. When these measures fail, each sought additional external props for self-containment, such as drugs, alcohol, sex, intense relationships, and other active distractions. There was a kind of surrender to the impoverishment of the inner world in Jim, resulting in a profound withdrawal from experiencing or feeling anything, as revealed, for example, by his retreat to France. According to the late psychoanalyst Erik Erikson, borderlines become "alienated" and detached. They try to isolate themselves from all the intolerable experiences of an internal emptiness and a disordered self by walling off all feelings. We think that this is how Jim must have felt at the end of his life. Others like Jim become resigned to the painful feelings of despair and develop a blank self, a numbing of all feeling experience except at a superficial level, giving others the impression of a shallow and peculiar personality. Janis on the other hand, was apparently struggling to survive even as she took that fatal dose of too-pure heroin and alcohol.

3. An incapacity to maintain stable, intimate relationships.

Our analysis points to the lives of Janis and Jim as revealing a clear pattern of **unstable, shifting relationships** with frequent, unpredictable alterations in emotional attachment or detachment. They appeared to lose personal boundaries while exhibiting such behaviors as clinging, avoiding, demanding, manipulating, and, at times, some combination of these. Their behaviors became increasingly Jekyl and Hyde-like, with sudden changes in mood, from being irrationally irritable to overtly hostile, as though they were trying to provoke a fight or some other extreme reaction. Like others in the dead zone, a kind of consuming, primitive hunger develops, making it possible for others to sexually or emotionally enslave them. These patients manifest a desperate need for emotional relatedness complicated by an intolerance for the frustrations inevitable in relationships and by the fear of abandonment, envelopment, or disappointment (otherwise known among clinicians as the "need-fear" dilemma). Dead Zone inhabitants often use people and things as "transitional" soothing objects like teddy bears or other toys. The person or thing selected may have no real existence of his/her own, but may exist only to gratify the individual's needs and reduce the tension created by life in the dead zone. For Janis and Jim, these relationships are usually symbiotic, dependent, narcissistic, or exploitative, and cannot be mutually gratifying or satisfying.

The Core of the Disturbance

The essence of the disturbance is currently being clarified by clinical concepts emerging from psychoanalytic research such as *splitting* and *object constancy*. Hoping to avoid making our discussion too technical, we will refer to splitting as a weakness in a person's ability to integrate the different sides of himself or different sides of others into one complex whole personality. Thus, to Janis and Jim, the same spouse or lover appeared to be ever shifting in his or her essence: one day good, helpful, and gratifying, the next day hostile, frustrating and rejecting.

The differing and sometimes contradictory sides we all possess are experienced by the person in the dead zone as separate and distinct personalities, though not in the sense that the term schizoid connotes. It is as if the friend or spouse is not the same person all the time and cannot be trusted, is not reliable or consistent. Such a misperception of a constantly changing interpersonal environment leaves the patient vulnerable to high anxiety, anger, black/white thinking, inconsistency, confusion, erratic functioning, and defensiveness.

Object constancy is the ability of patients to access internal images of important people in their lives, and/or to have any feelings about those images. Possession of this ability allows one to feel connected to others, to feel real and to be able to soothe oneself. In contrast, patients living in the dead zone have poor object constancy, understood as having no people (images or representations) to access or relate to. That's precisely why they feel so empty and desperately alone—and so would any of us, under those conditions.

The consequences of splitting and object inconstancy are also revealed in other areas of life such as work or school, where one's capacity to focus and perform is crucial. Despite being highly intelligent, Janice and Jim were academically inconsistent and remarkably unproductive, revealing a failure to engage in any sustained intellectual effort in these settings. They were unable to organize their mental resources for an extended period toward any goal requiring intellectual persistence and discipline. For example, they often experience great disparities in school or in interpersonal exchanges, good work performance but chaotic personal relations, good sexual functioning but poor personal relations. While Janis and Jim could be utterly amazing in concert, they were unable to function consistently within and between the various domains of daily life (education, career, and interpersonal relations).

Dead zone inhabitants also tend to be somewhat primitive. They are strongly inclined to the instantaneous present, so that when difficulties arise in important personal relationships they become revisionists (they remember things poorly). Clinicians label them as *unintegrated.* A multitude of good experiences in a relationship can be quickly forgotten in the context of some real or imagined but trivial slight by the partner, spouse, lover, or friend. Jim's outrageously stormy and volatile love/hate relationship with Pamela Courson is one good example. His many abuses of that relationship, his frequently angry exchanges with her leading to his detachment from her, usually resulted in emotional confusion, acting out, drinking without control (Jim almost always drank to get drunk), followed by episodes of anxiousness and quiet reconciliation. Always on alert status and lacking a sense of proportion in private matters, Janis and Jim possessed precious little capacity to absorb softer feelings, to soothe themselves.

Though the criteria cited above are generally useful in recognizing the disorder that took the lives of both Janis and Jim, the condition was only just beginning to be understood in the late Sixties and Seventies, and it would be another decade before clinicians would be sufficiently familiar with the patterns to have treatments available. Therefore, no one was really in a position to recognize the disorder while Janis and Jim were alive.

The Common Elements Of The Dead Zone

Two Dimensions can be employed to organize the confusing information about the dead zone in order to identify the more common features and escape the distraction of variations in behavior and personality. We have chosen to present the common elements of the disorder as succinctly as possible with two over-arching dimensions as a guide. In doing so, we hope to avoid discouraging the reader by rendering descriptions that are too technical or otherwise confusing. One dimension is the *level of functioning* and the other is the *emotive vs. the detached* dimension.

Level of functioning refers to how well such individuals can maintain themselves in a work or education environment, how well they can present themselves in the social milieu, how well they can engage in human relations, and how well they can contain the ordinary stresses of life without a deterioration in their reality testing. For example, higher level individuals with this condition, living in more safe, structured environments with support systems and reasonably collaborative partners, will most likely have better social relations and more resistance to slippage in reality testing under stress than lower level ones. The more severely disordered individuals will be more vulnerable to breakdowns requiring hospitalization, will have more chaotic relationships or none, and will eventually manifest more of the non-specific symptoms, such as erratic and unstable patterns of behavior, less tolerance for anxiety, more acting out to relieve inner tension, more clinging, more highly dependent and ambivalent relationships, greater fear of abandonment, panic attacks, greater impulsivity, increased likelihood of dissociative experiences, anorexia, bulimia, alcoholism and drug abuse. Viewing the lives of Janis and Jim with this newly constructed criterion, it is our judgment that they functioned at a *moderate* level of disorder.

The **emotive vs. detached** dimension refers to the differences among individuals in the degree of emotional expression and communication. On the one hand, highly emotive types, like

Janis, may *act out* whenever they feel any of the inner tension associated with life in the dead zone. They often create chaotic turbulence in the environment while expressing neediness and demanding attention. On the other hand, detached types do not so readily exhibit emotional lability (except under stress), seem to keep more to themselves, and frequently appear to be more distant. Jim appears to have possessed characteristics of both types, withdrawn and alone for long periods of time, followed by emotionally engaged episodes in which he created great turbulence. Despite his episodes of impulsivity, he was just as likely to seek resolution of the same inner conflicts and tensions associated with life in the dead zone by an emotional withdrawal and avoidance of real relationships. In Jim's case, though his behavior appeared more outwardly controlled at times, and he was *detached* from any true connection to others, habitually engaging in transient, superficial relationships bereft of emotional investment.

W. W. Meissner has conceptualized these types as constituting a "spectrum," placing Janis on the "hysterical continuum," and Jim on the "schizoid continuum." He has unscrambled some of the confusion resulting from the wide differences in outward behavior among such personalities by identifying and describing the two dimensions of hysterical and schizoid, and by describing them in terms of higher order, the middle and lower order personality functioning described above (Meissner 1984, chp. 1). Thus we can now think of these disorders as having degrees of disturbance from severe through moderate to mild. We can also think of some of them as having degrees of emotionality, attachment, and outward turbulence, ranging from high to low. What this means for us is that people living in the dead zone present a number of complex behaviors, exhibiting the symptoms of the disorder to various degrees and through a variety of characteristics.

People with this condition have a long history of mild to moderate symptoms and atypical or unusual behaviors beginning in childhood or early adolescence (though many of the problem behaviors are also common to several other psychological

13

conditions). They do not all manifest the same degree of acting-out behavior, paranoid tendencies, narcissistic traits, overt emotionality, hostility, antisocial attitudes, and vulnerability to drugs and alcohol. Nevertheless there are certain observable behavior patterns, signs, and symptoms that are common to this condition, transcending the confusing differences in personality style and nonspecific signs and symptoms.

Chapter Two: Janis And Jim—Popular Accounts And Misconceptions

From childhood's hour I have
not been as others were.
I have not seen as others saw.

from "Alone" by Edgar Allen Poe

By most accounts, they were the king and queen of rock and roll in the Sixties, and both died at age twenty-seven due to the abuse they had visited upon themselves. A generation heard Morrison's call to "break on through" and Joplin's cry that "you know you've got it if it makes you feel good." When an interviewer asked Janis what she thought young people wanted she replied, "sincerity and a good time." There is no record of any Jim Morrison answer to such a question, but we can be reasonably sure (based on biographical information available to us) it would have been esoteric and dark.

They were both born around the same time to conventional, white southern families. Both were very intelligent, given to outrageous behaviors in high school, and rejected by most of their classmates. Both were narcissistic, rebellious, anti-authoritarian, and intensely needy, and they exhibited severely conflicted inner selves. While Morrison was seen as an unpredictable Jekyll and Hyde, Joplin had much more of a go-for-broke, roller coaster-like unpredictability. They knew each other, liked each other's work, were lovers for a while.

All the biographical accounts report that they once met at a party, which was noteworthy only because Janis ended up slugging Jim on the head with a whiskey bottle for behaving in his typically obnoxious way. Neither initially sought fame or even the status of a rock singer. They simply hung out with the boys. Neither could contain disruptive impulses or maintain non-exploitative or non-abusive relationships, and, of course, as we will show, both were consumed by the relentless inner

16

desolateness of the *dead zone*. Both abused drugs and alcohol throughout their adult lives and engaged in endless rounds of chaotic relationships that left much emotional debris in their wakes. Sadly, the best adjectives we can think of to describe the progress of their lives is self-destructive and anarchic.

The similarities go further. Both Janis and Jim were highly intelligent with clearly superior IQ's. Despite a maverick status in school, each read and absorbed quality literature and had a natural proficiency with language. According to his biographers, Riordan and Prochnicky (1991), Morrison had a recorded IQ of 149. Janis's superior intelligence was manifested in verbal skills, a quick wit, and a familiarity with good literature. One has only to watch those engaging interviews in the documentary "Janis" to confirm her mental agility in give and take situations, and her latent intellectual capacity.

Jim also read extensively on many dark and arcane subjects, wrote poems of arguably publishable quality, and struggled with existential issues both in verbal and written form through his music and writings. He and Janis were both multi-talented. A precocious child, Janis frequently demonstrated above average ability in art and drawing, and later in vocalizing and interpreting music, composing songs spontaneously off the top of her head. Jim's writings and poems are surreal and quite obscure, but clearly authored with intelligence and intense feeling by one with an obvious talent for vocalizing and writing songs. Each had an electric effect on their audiences that has rarely been matched in intensity and in longevity. People who have been to a Joplin or Morrison concert recall the experience with amazing clarity and enthusiasm twenty-five years later.

What was not widely known, however, is that both suffered greatly from a highly disorganized emotional life. This rather uncommon disorganization is experienced by many as an emptiness which leaves them without the capacity to take in and feel the soothing that comes from attachments to others. It is a despair that is felt every waking moment by those who unintentionally find themselves struggling with the necessity of living a life in the emotional black hole of the dead zone.

Popular Misconceptions

The pathos of their lives and the tragedy of their deaths invites a kind of easy speculation about causes. Relatives, biographers, and fans have considered the possibilities and offered their speculations which generally fall into one or more of the following hypotheses.

The first is that the subculture of substance abuse destroyed them; that Janis and Jim were overtaken by the fast-paced excitement and demands of rock star life. Drug and alcohol abuse were so pervasively a part of that life that they were inexorably drawn in and became what would be called today chemically dependent, a condition from which they were unable to escape. Each died from either a drug overdose or from a lethal combination of drugs and alcohol.

That other great talents who performed in this era also died under similar circumstance is a matter of historical record: Jimi Hendrix, Elvis Presley, Marilyn Monroe, Judy Garland and John Belushi. Most recently in April, 1994, Kurt Cobain, lead singer for the group *Nirvana* killed himself with a shotgun blast after years of drug abuse. His suicide came only a few months after River Phoenix died from complications of drug overdose.

The public knowledge of and attitude toward drugs was different in the Sixties. The counterculture to which Janis and Jim belonged encouraged the use of drugs to liberate one from stultifying convention and to "expand one's mind." This was a time when gurus such as Timothy Leary recommended the use of mind altering drugs such as LSD, and when the medical profession for the most part ignored the extensive use of amphetamines by film stars, apparently acquiescing to the demands of a subculture that would not be denied any pleasure or experience.

On this line, then, performing artists, musicians, and their ilk frequently indulged in drugs and alcohol abuse, a widely accepted and understood feature of their environment (though the effects were not fully understood). Can the trajectory of the lives of Janis and Jim, then, be explained by pointing to their chemical dependence on drugs and alcohol, moving them so quickly into the self-destructive behaviors that eventually killed them?

It is perhaps easier to understand why this hypothesis has so many proponents than why it is, nonetheless, a misconception about the two. The list of drug-related deaths among entertainers is long, and the use of drugs for relief of stress by many show business people has a well documented history. When we note the more casual attitude toward drug use during the Sixties—the general ignorance about the addictive nature of some drugs and the popular practice of combining drugs—the possibility of being "caught up" in the drug scene is eminently believable.

However, this hypothesis raises more questions than it answers. For instance, what of the well documented feelings of alienation and despair the two repeatedly voiced long before drugs and alcohol became so pervasive in their lives? If one takes the view then that the ingrained drug culture of the entertainment world pushed Janis and Jim into their graves, how can we account for their distressing behaviors when they were not on drugs or using alcohol? There were periods when they weren't using drugs or alcohol, and yet they still exhibited impulsive, crude, and self-destructive behaviors. The problem here is that any connection between the substance abuse and their notorious behavior is extremely difficult to establish. Under these circumstances, to posit a cause and effect relation between the abuse and their self-destructive behavior is simply wrong.

A second problem with this hypothesis is that it does not account for the fact that these two people engaged in self-destructive behaviors when they were adolescents. According to their biographers, who provide lengthy accounts of the childhood and adolescent behaviors of Janis and Jim, their early histories were very much like their adult behaviors. One need not be a clinician to recognize the presence of an emotional disorder after reading of Janis' teenage excesses in Myra Friedman's biography, *Buried Alive*, or in *Love, Janis,* a book by Janis' sister, Laura. According to Jim's biographers, this pattern held for him as well. No matter how detrimental drugs and alcohol became in their lives, it would be incorrect to assume that alcohol and drug abuse were anything but symptoms of something else, i.e., symptoms of deeper, less obvious disorders.

There are still other details of their lives which disconfirm this hypothesis. Despite the publicity that is given to the drug-related death of a star, the vast majority of performing artists do not die so early in their lives, nor do they engage in chaotic, self-destructive behaviors—though many might have had some experiences with drugs and alcohol. Elvis Presley and Jimi Hendrix for example, for all their abuse of various substances, did not behave in such aggressive and chaotic ways, nor did they verbalize the feelings of alienation and despair that was so characteristic of Janis and Jim. Again, it is quite clear that drugs and alcohol may have complicated the analysis of the lives of these two great personalities, but cannot alone explain their tragic lives.

A second hypothesis has to do with the idea that fame and fortune had a destructive effect on their egos with neither able to handle the pressure—pressure placed on otherwise stable personalities. On this line, then, the vicissitudes of fame and fortune rather than alcohol and drug abuse are offered as the cause. A Fifties movie, *A Face In The Crowd*, (in which a sudden rise to fame corrupted a previously decent and conventional guy) is less than a subtle dramatization of the perils of show business success. Those who propose this account wish us to believe that success in that competitively cruel and aggressive world of entertainment is actually a defeat for one's spiritual and emotional health. Especially important in this view is the idea that the star is continually exploited and increasingly alienated, finally turning to drugs and alcohol for relief. This theme is encountered in at least one biography of Marilyn Monroe, and is suggested in the movie based on Janis's life, *The Rose*. Thus either their egos are artificially pumped up from the fantastic rush and adoration of fans—setting them up for a fall— or they are manipulated and dehumanized by agents or directors so that they are pushed to exhaustion and demoralized.

It is taken as a given that the temptations of "big" money, the carnal pleasures, the fame and casual lifestyle of show business can ruin the hardiest of souls, and that the exploitation of Janis and Jim was so intense that it should not come as a surprise that their lives ended so. A rather widely held hypothesis, it has, in fact, a degree of validity, though perhaps only the appearance of respectability. The high divorce rates for big stars as well as their highly publicized use of drugs and alcohol offer support for this view.

Under close scrutiny, however, this popular speculation fails to make the required connection between the lifestyle and the deterioration in the performer's psychological health and general well being. The impressions gained from headline stories notwithstanding, the overwhelming majority of successful stars and show business people presumably subjected to the same pressures, do not become self-destructive, do not live chaotic public and private lives and, of course, do not die of drug overdoses. Janis and Jim experienced no more show business pressure than others who reached the same level of success. We emphasize this fact in spite of the great publicity given to the deaths of a *seemingly* large number of famous rock and Hollywood stars: Elvis, Hendrix, Monroe, Garland, Belushi, Kurt Cobain and so on. These deaths aside, many other stars had to cope with the pressures of stardom that were a constant source of aggravation in their lives, but which did not *cause* the inner conflicts that eventually destroyed them. Thus we must look further into the personalities themselves for the answers.

A third hypothesis may be summarized as follows: Great but tragic stars may have experienced something in their backgrounds, some trauma or particular family circumstance that shaped their personalities in ways leading to tragedy. Based on a distortion of Freudian/psychoanalytic perspectives that "the child is the father of the man," this view theorizes that what happens to a child during the developing years directly and indirectly determines the characteristics of the adult. For Janis, the speculation is that she had a cold and rigid mother and an unsympathetic family, that she was stifled and not allowed to be herself, forced to accept the parochial values of a conservative, religious southern town in the "suffocating" Fifties. Her acting out behaviors on this line are seen as a reactive search for her real self and a desire to be free and to be loved. It is regrettable, insist the proponents of this hypothesis, that she was unable to overcome those difficult "background" hindrances and was thus consumed by them.

In Jim's case, a particularly traumatic incident early in his childhood would provide the explanatory variable for his premature death when combined with a family characterization similar to Janis'.

Were Janis and Jim's childhood experiences responsible for their destruction? Were mom and/or dad too punitive, too rigid, too unavailable, too conventional, too controlling, too unemotional, too conflicted or too (you could easily fill in the rest with your view of parental failures)? Were there traumatic experiences?

Based on the wealth of good data from recorded interviews with both Janis and Jim, from the many biographies, and from anecdotal reports, this hypothesis is simply insupportable. To begin with, no record or anecdotal report has ever been found which supports the idea that either was mistreated as a child, nor is there any claim by Janis or Jim, themselves, that they were mistreated. In fact, just the opposite is true.

Although her parents could be classified as having conventional values, and perhaps being comfortably middle class, Janis's parents were portrayed by her biographers as tolerant of her attention-seeking, outrageous behaviors, encouraging of her intellectual and artistic interests, and deeply concerned about her well-being. Janis' sister, Laura, in her recent book, *Love Janis,* includes many letters and phone calls from Janis to her mother and family, and convincingly dispels any doubt about the strong bond between them. The same take about Janis and her family was presented by Myra Friedman twenty years earlier in *Buried Alive.*

That Janis' parents were concerned about her lifestyle and the frequent chemical abuse there is no doubt. Yet they remained supportive of and responsive to her throughout her life. We know of no biography of Janis that describes her parents as a problem to her in that way, nor of any other account of her life that confirms this glib and popular but mostly faulty hypothesis. Based on the reliable information currently available about Janis, it has no validity.

The same hypothesis fares no better when considering the life of Jim Morrison. Despite some dramatic conflicts with his parents over "values" and "attitude," and despite an outrageous pattern of misbehavior as a child, his family life was otherwise quite stable. His parents supported his endeavors and generally tolerated his difficult personality. Though Jim showed early signs of emotional problems—in contrast to Janis' who did not—his family was neither hostile toward him nor considered dysfunctional in the conventional use of the term. His later attitudes of hostility toward them is better understood as a consequence of his inner struggle with the dead zone. So while Jim was temperamentally difficult (as was Janis, given the available evidence) we simply cannot attribute his emotional conflicts to a dysfunctional or abusive family.

When speculation about Jim's family is not the basis for explaining his life, other popular accounts focus on a childhood experience he had at the age of four while traveling with his parents in their car. There was reportedly a serious automobile accident, the aftermath of which left the passengers (Navaho Indians) bloodied and suffering greatly. Morrison later verbalized about the accident a great deal and its affect on him. Many have hypothesized that young Jim was traumatized by the incident, affecting his life from that day forward. As a kind of postscript to that hypothesis, it is alleged that his family was lorded over by his father, a naval officer and aircraft carrier commander who was reportedly rigid and controlling.

In *Break On Through,* Riordan and Prochnicky suggest that some people thought that Morrison suffered deep psychological trauma from that incident. They cite the findings of parapsychologists who, after looking into the details of the accident, describe the possibility that Morrison was possessed by the souls of the dying Indians. Morrison frequently described this incident in rich detail, possibly supporting the claim that he was so shaken that he was unable to continue his life in any normal way. His subsequent on-stage Indian Shaman-like dancing appears rooted in this early experience, according to those subscribing to this hypothesis.

But to suppose that he drank to quiet the demons that invaded him at the accident scene, or that he was possessed by the souls of the dead, is to engage in nothing more than a highly speculative exercise aimed at explaining Jim's life and death by looking to supernatural explanations. This account, of course, is completely unwarranted. Why don't others who experience a particularly gruesome accident exhibit the peculiar behaviors and antics that characterized Jim's life? Methodologically, the easy hypothesis of early childhood trauma is as unable to establish a connection between the incident and his disorder. The hypothesis represents bad science in that selective episodes from his childhood are used in an ad hoc and post hoc manner to account for his disturbing and self defeating behaviors.

Finally, a more recent hypothesis, emerging from the increasing recognition of the prevalence of depressive disorders in the general population, suggests that Janis and Jim suffered from undiagnosed major depression. The alcohol and drug abuse that so characterized their desperate lives is seen as a consequence of this untreated clinical condition. This hypothesis, while certainly explaining the suicides of many public figures, does not fit Janis or Jim. Neither had exhibited the basic symptoms of a major depression such as constant fatigue or loss of energy, diminished ability to think or concentrate, an overtly depressed mood, markedly diminished interest or pleasure in most activities most of the time, reoccurring insomnia or hypersomnia almost daily, and psycho-motor retardation or agitation. One who is depressed experiences life with apathy, strains to carry on with life, is usually consumed with feelings of guilt or self-reproach and a sense of loss and longing.

Using these as significant criteria, we would be hard pressed to claim either Janis or Jim as having suffered from depression. In fact, to any of their biographers, to their close friends and relatives, and, of course, to experienced clinicians, nothing was further from the truth about their lives. None of these biographers has ever suggested depression. So that hypothesis cannot offer a plausible account of their mutual misery anymore than the previous two hypotheses could.

What then can we say about the these highly popularized and glib accounts of the causes of Janis and Jim's self-destructive lives? Methodologically flawed, extravagantly speculative, often at odds with reputable evidence, and marked by rudimentary applications of modern clinical diagnostic categories, such "explanations" should be easily dismissed. Regrettably, they have persisted for far too long. We now have available to us more substantial explanations such as those drawn from enriched descriptive categories rooted in what clinicians now term *borderline disorders.*

We take it to be a major concern of this book to describe Janis and Jim by applying the current clinical understandings of these disorders in order to offer revealing accounts of what actually happened to them. The advances of psychology and psychiatry over the past twenty or so years since the deaths of Janis and Jim provide us with a qualitatively different picture of the two. If they had the benefit of therapy rooted in these recent insights, both might have survived. Our hope now is that others so afflicted may be diagnosed and treated in a more timely manner.

Chapter Three: Janis Joplin, A Woman Left Lonely

"Take another little piece of my heart
now baby, You know you've got it, if
it makes you feel good . . . ."

Perhaps no modern figure embodied the characteristic features of the borderline personality or is more familiar with life in that dead zone than Janis Joplin. Remarkably extravagant, often witty and crude, highly emotional yet creative and intelligent, she affords us now, some twenty years after her death, the opportunity to perform a psychological postmortem. While we hope to demonstrate that she could easily be diagnosed as a borderline personality type, as one who lived her life in that *dead zone*, we also hope to reveal that she was more than the sum of her anarchic frames of mind.

Whether in biographies reviewing her life or in documentary film interviews with her, Janis consistently presents as a high energy, extremely talented, sharply humorous personality. The life of Janis Joplin is described in all her exuberance in a biography by Myra Friedman. In it we are presented with an extraordinary portrait "written with a sympathetic intelligence, and at times a fiercely lyrical voice." As astonishing and revealing as Friedman's account is, however, the actual interviews with Janis shown in a documentary offer the interested analyst a dazzling array of the symptomatic features now associated with borderline personalities.

In *Janis,* the film producers captured a smiling, wisecracking, hopelessly unintegrated, anxious, very lonely woman who sang with that overwhelmingly powerful and emotionally breathtaking voice; one who had a cackling laugh, who dressed outlandishly in feathers and a boa and who had a propensity to overuse Sixties slang such as *cat, man, dude and right on momma.* She was indeed the Janis we had imagined after reading *Buried Alive.*

As our research into her life progressed, we were as much

fascinated as educated, in that our interest in understanding and evaluating her began to engender a growing sense of sadness and empathy for the torment she endured. We became more engrossed as well in the powerful emotional forces expressed in her singing. Friends of ours who had once seen Janis in concert recall her electrifying performance: the music, the audience reaction, the shock to the system and the explosion of emotional energy that filled everyone with wild abandonment, with very intense feelings was followed by a "washed out" affect. Listening to Janis sing, it was difficult to believe the claim made by some who knew her very early, that her voice was fuller and more powerful before she became famous.

In the same film documentary Janis was interviewed a number of times—once on *The Dick Cavett Show,* later at a reunion in her home town, and while on a European tour. On the Cavett show she was clearly in top form, trading wisecracks and easily outclassing the dapper Cavett in repartee. Friedman writes of a later appearance in which it was clear that Janis was losing her struggle with those dark inner forces over which she had so little control. Subsequent interviews with her exposed an underlying fragility, that of a confused little girl valiantly trying to maintain a crumbling intrapsychic balance by adopting the extremes of the Sixties counterculture for support.

In our effort to reconstruct Janis' psychology, we necessarily turned to her talented and thorough biographers, two of whom had lived with her (Laura Joplin, Myra Friedman), and to films of her performances and interviews. In addition, we extrapolated from the reactions of those people old enough to have seen her in concert and from the exclamations of her many current young fans who know her only through her reissued music. From the vantage point of the clinician, however, Janis sounded and acted like many patients who have also felt the terrible desolation of life in that dead zone.

How can we comprehend the life of this intense young woman, uniquely talented but consumed by such extreme emotions and a self-destructive capacity? How can the pathos of her life be understood? What accounts for her excesses, her drug and alcohol abuse, and her irrational behaviors?

Was she really any different from the numerous artists, writers, rock stars and political figures who self-destructed, such as Jimi Hendrix, Elvis Presley, John Belushi, Marilyn Monroe, Sylvia Plath, Ernest Hemingway, James Forrestal, Vince Foster, River Phoenix and Kurt Cobain? To respond to that question we must examine the many details of her life, seeking to explain her state of mind as she coped with the emptiness of the dead zone.

Background

According to her biographers, Janis Joplin was born to a proper, middle class, bible belt family in Port Arthur, Texas in 1943. In *Pearl: The Obsessions and Passions of Janis Joplin* (1992), Ellis Amburn (1992) describes Mrs. Joplin as conventional but bright woman, a bit of a maverick in her own right, and musically talented.

Laura Joplin writes that her mother was an energetic, musical, attentive mother, always a creative parent, always energized in teaching her children. Mrs. Joplin bought Janis a piano and taught her how to play, exposed all her children to music, gourmet cooking, artistic and creative activities, and engaged in many traditional pursuits such as preparing holiday feasts, baking cookies, and making Christmas decorations. Laura Joplin describes her mother as the best teacher she ever knew, that learning from her was a daily experience.

Mrs. Joplin was the organizer of her children's' daily lives, a creative spirit who taught her children songs and generally inspired them to learn. Her family was more philosophically liberal than the Port Arthur community, despite otherwise observing its conventional standards. Janis frequently telephoned her mother over the years seeking reassurance and maintaining contact. All the major biographers describe the presence of a loving relationship between mother and daughter in spite of Janis's excesses and outrageous adolescent behavior.

Janis' biographers all point to the strong and loving attachment she had to her father. He was a fun loving, intelligent man who was well loved by his children and who truly loved them. He was a playful engineer and tinkerer who created unusual swings, seesaws, and toys for his children. Like his wife, he valued thinking and learning, always encouraging the children to participate in dinner table discussions on many books, ideas, and music.

He managed to find creative activities for his children even in the limited cultural environment of Port Arthur. For example, he would take them to the post office to look at the wanted posters and to the library where he would advise them about reading material. Laura Joplin recounts how he:

> . . . was especially ingenious at getting the gang of kid to help with the chores. Like Tom Sawyer trying to get the fence painted, he invited everyone over to help wax the oak floors. He cleaned out the living room and dining room and spread the floor with wax. Then he took any number of dirty bare feet and strapped clean towels on them. Off he would send us to skate and play bumper cars on the glass-like surface the new wax created. We never had so much fun (Joplin 1992, 32)

Laura Joplin noted that her parents were very concerned about Janis' tendency to react so negatively to community values and standards that she was often hated and ridiculed. Although the Joplin family was apparently more liberal than the community on civil rights, for example, they managed to conform to local norms when they didn't seriously conflict with commitments of that sort. They cajoled, lectured, and finally set limits on her strange behaviors in a effort to help her fit in. "Please don't set the world against you," Janis was often advised. When all else failed they sent her to a counselor and even considered family therapy at one point.

Thus, based on the many accounts, letters and interviews available since Janis's death, it is difficult to escape the conclusion that she came from a stable, secure, and emotionally supportive family, and that her early childhood years at least were peaceful and happy. And there is still more to learn from her biographers who all corroborate the details of her family life.

From Myra Friedman, Laura Joplin, and Ellis Amburn, we learn that Janis was a shy child, cooperative and easy to raise, cheerful and very normal. Janis' mother is quoted as saying that as a child, Janis did exceptional school work, was accelerated in the third grade, had no behavior difficulties, and never did anything deserving correction. Remarking once that Janis did need more attention than other children, her mother describes her as "unhappy and unsatisfied without it." In interviews with her biographers, Janis consistently recalled her childhood as nearly idyllic.

Janis' adolescence, however, received no such label. As Janis said "then the whole world turned, it just turned on me. " According to Amburn, Janis became unpopular in high school, a wallflower early on, not very pretty, and plagued by an overweight condition and serious acne. She slowly developed outrageous, provocative behaviors throughout her high school years, later becoming the first "beatnik" in that unappreciative town. Acting-out and engaging in wild, unusual, and strange behaviors, she had a "foul mouth", ran with others so inclined, expected to get her own way, and would try anything. Some called her a "slut" and "pig," often throwing pennies at her as a sign of disrespect. By the time she arrived at junior high school, Janis was belligerent, frequently expressing her ideas in a strident voice while showing off her abrasive and alienating lifestyle. She was also astonishingly naive, gullible, and impressionable (Amburn 1992, 14).

Apparently narcissistic, stubborn, thrill-seeking, and trashy, her activities at age fourteen would be diagnosed today as *conduct disordered*, the hallmarks being early sexual promiscuity, hanging out with hoodlums, emotionally hyper reactive, impulsive and erratic behavior. She was unpredictable, often took dangerous risks, and showed up drunk for graduation. Amburn felt that "something underlying in Janis put her in destructive situations" (Amburn 1992, 1-35). Not simply rebellious, Janis craved acceptance, had a great need to exhibit herself, and had almost no control over her impulses as she got older. She read voluminously, had a strong mind and intellect, was talented in art and music, and had a kind heart, yet she never lived up to her potential.

While a senior in high school, she managed to insert herself into a sophisticated group of very talented male musicians, becoming "one of the boys." After graduation, Janis just knocked around, drinking a lot and having fun. Shortly thereafter she spent some time in a psychiatric hospital for a condition she later alluded to as a nervous breakdown. She rose to fame during that rather peculiar historical period known as the turbulent Sixties, a time when many were intent on loosening moral and political rigidities of an earlier era. Rebellious and irreverent, the major countercultural figures from that decade exerted such an irresistible pull on her that she soon found a home among people championing the emerging forces of change in San Francisco's Haight-Ashbury neighborhood.

In that milieu, Janis first learned to live on the edge, and while there, to create a life of artistic excitement, incessant turbulence and chaos. Thus one should not be surprised that she completely embraced the subculture of "sex, drugs and rock and roll." Friedman writes, "Attending her concerts was like mainlining an aphrodisiac right through the spine." It was in that unalterably "wired" environment that Janis attempted to engage life, hoping to find the feeling she could not experience in the dead zone. Perhaps best expressed in her song "*Try*," she persistently sought what she had been unable to feel. She often said she wouldn't sing any song she didn't feel, that she made no separation between her professional and personal life. Clearly she remained hopeful longer than most who find themselves residents of the dead zone; clearly her behavior revealed how

31

desperately she searched for the way out.

Trying Just A Little Bit Harder: Managing Life In The Dead Zone

Tryiuh, oh yeah, Tryiuh, oh yeah
Just a little bit harder . . . .

Janis' biographers all provide rich descriptive accounts of the effects that drugs and alcohol had on her, and of how tumultuous and disordered her life became in the process. Accurately describing how drug abuse can dull the senses, Janis' sister wrote that "it appeals to people with an unquenchable inner turmoil (Joplin 1992,). . . All Janis wanted was dope, any dope, to smoke dope, take dope, lick dope, suck dope, fuck dope" (Friedman 1992, 48). She also noticed that her sister "was never interested in psychedelics . . . since psychedelics only intensify experience." Asked by a friend once why she did dope, Janis replied "I just want a little fucking peace, man" (Friedman 1992, 49).

Peace from what one might ask? Perhaps she sought peace from the unrelenting dread, a dread known only to those who experience life peering through the distorting lens within the dead zone.

It is important, here to distinguish the account of Janis' drug and alcohol use, provided by her sister and biographers and accepted by many of her followers from the deeper explanation we offer in this book. We believe it to be crucial to a proper diagnosis of her disorder to separate the symptom from the cause, to understand that the depression Janis experienced after and between concerts was mainly symptomatic of a kind of battle fatigue suffered in her tragic war against the constant sense of emptiness she felt. To substantiate that claim, we must first examine the accounts of her heroin use, beginning with her sister, Laura's version.

Janis, Laura noted, reversed the standard practice of most heroin abusers by using heroin *after* the thrill of a successful concert. Speculating that Janis wasn't trying to escape the psychological pain of life circumstances, she suggests instead that Janis was using heroin to avoid the depression which often follows the high of supercharged concerts, much the way a speed freak would smooth re-entry into daily life. To say the least, Janis' performances were always emotionally intense, never failing to move the audience to the apex of arousal. In her sister's view, then, Janis' heroin use was meant to help ease her way down from the adrenaline high stimulated by her performances, to facilitate emotional movement from the hysterical high of the stage to a normal level of everyday living (Joplin 1992,).

It is now conventionally understood that Janis' reliance on heroin for the reason suggested by her sister might appear to be plausible and sustainable. However, that view at best only obscures Janis' emotional condition at the time. While many entertainers require a cooling down period after performances, much as a runner does after a race, most don't employ drugs to do so, nor do many require ingesting both drugs and alcohol in the same amounts as Janis did. In addition, after the concerts are over, one isn't likely to find such entertainers continually using the two as intensely as Janis did, unless one is prepared to lengthen substantially the calming down time. Or, to put this differently, one should be able to observe Janis during a calm period following the use of drugs, and yet that doesn't appear to be characteristic of her in her after performance binges.

Like so many patients who experience the "incoherent dread" every waking moment, Janis too would try anything to fill the dead zone with the energy of life she derived from frenetic, uncontrolled interaction with those around her. One might easily be exhausted and overwhelmed by the intensity of the hour-by-hour experiences in her daily life. Her unpredictable shifts in mood, thrill-seeking behavior, persistent alcohol and drug abuse, lack of impulse control, sexual obsessions, and emotionally powerful performances in concert were mostly futile efforts at escape, not from depression, but from the "private madness" to which she was driven by that inevitable inner deadness that encompassed her.

We believe that Janis took heroin or alcohol after concerts because they numbed the senses, helping to mask her awareness of the returning torment of emptiness, of the void that attacked her spirit and ultimately sapped her will to live. Thus, she did not suffer from depression except perhaps secondarily. Typically depressive people who use drugs look for a lift, a mood elevator like cocaine, not heroin. Rather it was the emptiness hidden beneath the speedy and hypnotic action of a Janis Joplin concert that had to be managed later by "sex, drugs and rock and roll." Her post-concert drug use was no different from her behaviors at any other time she had to face the terrifying experiences of her own inner world.

Her need to manage the nightmare of the void within, a terrifying loneliness unknown and unfathomable to most, also explains Janis' incessant thrill-seeking, absurd sexual posturing, and sexual adventurism. Janis was forever talking about, bragging about, or seeking sexual activity. Films of her singing and talking to the audience and filmed interviews in which she frequently makes crude sexual references and asides such as "getting it" and "doing it" appear to confirm this judgment. Many of her most outrageous behaviors and eccentricities appear in retrospect (and we might add, after twenty-five years of clinical discoveries and experiences) to have been aspects of her basic personality which also served to deflect, diminish, and deter the demons of the dead zone. Only in highly energized states of being generated by sex, drugs, performing in concert, and partying could she find some temporary relief, or "a little fucking peace, man."

Her principal biographer, former publicist, companion, and friend, Myra Friedman (1973), wrote the most psychologically sophisticated, penetrating and emotionally wrenching account of Janis' life. Friedman described one exchange with an increasingly fragmented Janis who expressed that it wasn't "in the cards" for her to have better relationships, that she was doomed to experience only transient and therefore unfulfilling relations. Disagreeing and pointing out the many opportunities

Janis had, Friedman heard Janis reply sadly "Well, I know, but I get so lonely and it seems like I'm driven and I don't know, I just do things and I don't know why" (Friedman 1973, 56). Clinicians familiar with patients living in the dead zone, however, do know *why*, though they have only recently come to understand the special agony Janis experienced.

Searching For Love: Me And Bobby McGee

From a clinical perspective, Janis' preoccupation with sex can easily be explained as her attempt to "manage the dread", and as subsequently revealing the difficulty she had with what psychoanalysts call "object relations."

Read how Friedman describes this phenomenon, albeit in a less technical way:

> Janis was consumed and driven by a need for love that was preposterous in its magnitude, her excessive narcissism the result of bitter frustrations and the very stuff of her insecurity, her desire for constant attention and her gluttonous hunger for approval. She was fanatical in pursuit of affection while rendered incapable, by the self-direction of her feelings, of establishing intimate relationships. Like a longing child crying for love, her aim was to receive, to take into herself a comforting warmth of which, for whatever reasons, she felt acutely deprived. With an obsessive and insatiable need such as that, what sex would fill it became a secondary matter and the physical demonstration of affection a substitute gratification for what she essentially craved (Friedman 1973, 61).

35

Later, Friedman expands on her explanation for Janis' crude, overt sexual behavior on stage and everywhere and the bravado exaggerations of her sexual escapades:

> But Janis breathed, thought, felt, acted at a primitive level that was nearly absolute. Even in her twenties, she was still like a hurt and pleading child who wants exactly that very love complete in the physical embrace, and sex, in a way, was a valid synonym for what she was in search of (Friedman 1973, 125).

We take this account to be another example of the desperate search for the "love," a search for missing internal objects, i.e., mental "representations" of the essential people we all must have stored in us to feel "real," secure, filled up, and soothed. It is nothing less than the search for the primitive mother, the mother of infancy who could calm all anxieties and bring the soothing that the child cannot bring to itself. Without the capacity to develop and hold on to these internal representations of the mother, the child is left totally alone in an empty internal world, to struggle interminably with a relentless "object hunger" that cannot be satisfied. Again, Friedman is quite helpful in capturing what love meant for Janis:

> It wasn't love as an adult knows it: no sharing, no interest, no commitment, no giving, none of those things at all. But it really was love to her. In her hunger for affection, she was nearly amok. Her constant pursuit of physical contact resonated with echoes of infant longing, and frustration of such a need could not help but produce an unbearable anxiety. In that sense, sex was a palliative, an

escape from tension that could not be
endured, thus making sexual relief of
inordinate, overbearing importance"
(Friedman 1973, 128).

In part, she was a lost child with talent, who could not sustain
any long term, non-exploitative relationship, and who acted
primarily on narcissistic needs and impulses. Janis' unbearable
anxiety came from her life in the dead zone and it prevented the
growth and maturation of her personality so necessary for stable
and satisfying object relations. She tended to experience others,
in the way that Friedman describes, as a child would. Her
intimate relations would always be unstable and tumultuous.

Friedman points out how Janis wouldn't sing anything that
didn't fit her feelings. In one interview from the film
documentary, *Janis*, she tells the interviewer that she did not
have a private life different from her performing life. Thus we
look at her lyrics and find confirmation of the "search for the
object," a search doomed to failure because she had no capacity
to experience the object (person) in a satisfying way. Consider
any one of the titles of her songs. Although they are hopeful,
they expected disappointment.

Try	Ball And Chain
One Good Man	Half Moon
Down On Me	Get It While You Can
Cry	I Need A Man To Love
Piece Of My Heart	A Woman Left Lonely
Bye, Bye Baby	Little Girl Blue
No Reason For Livin	Buried Alive In The Blues
Move Over	Women Is Losers
Me And Bobby McGee	All Is Loneliness

One can hardly find a title from her works that doesn't suggest
that "need." And we should recall that she insisted she wouldn't
sing any song she didn't feel.

Searching For Janis: Nothing Left To Lose

Another aspect of life in the dead zone is the presence of a markedly distorted or unstable sense of self. Here again Friedman portrays Janis:

> Janis was swamped in her own pizzazz and amplification quite apart from a word of print or even her stage performances. In that bellowing, bouncing, jangling clamor, there were those who saw a 'self.' But Janis was afflicted by an emotional astigmatism. Each second was clear but there was no focus. She was disordered, decentralized and diffused (Friedman 1973, 129).

These insightful observations of her close friend, colleague, and principle biographer are consistent with the narcissistic, tension filled actions and experiences of someone who lacks an "inner cohesion" and a stable identity.

Characteristically, those who live in the dead zone develop a diffuse and unfocused self which, in Janis' case, left her struggling to find something at the core of her being, something that might rectify the blurred and unsteady perception of herself. She adopted first one then another identity, either dramatic or symbolic (victim, tough guy, sex queen, party animal, anti-establishment heroine, rock star, and so on). The significant consequence for Janis was a unique kind of intolerable psychic tension.

One example of her quickly shifting identity experiments can be found in her decision to take a new name, "Pearl." The poetic irony of this new identity was not lost on Friedman who describes Janis' agony by penetrating the surface explanation:

> But Pearl was another story, a

hard-drinking-swearing-always-partying-f
uck-anybody-get-it-on-get-it-off-stay-ston
ed-keep-on-rocking-floozy, flourishing
under the tyranny of an applause that
didn't come just from the galleries. And
still, lurking like an amorphous ghost
behind that public persona, there was
another Janis, in that last year asserting
herself in equally clear definition, but
thriving in an isolation as deeply painful
as the most solitary of prison
confinements (Friedman 1973, 220).

Finding the "Pearl business just too eerie," Friedman observes
that, "The schism in her personality was quite visible enough,
exceeding anything that could be construed as the common
contradictions in human nature."

If her biographers' descriptions are accurate, Janis had no
true sense of herself as a person, woman, or partner. The
disturbed self-concept so characteristic of people living in the
dead zone and so obvious to experienced clinicians today left
Janis aimless and lost, always seeking to feel she belonged
somewhere. Underlying her insistent claim of uniqueness there
was, however, a recognizable person.

None of these "identities" gave her what she so desperately
needed: a stable, cohesive sense of herself with the capacity to
soothe herself and quiet the inner discord. Reflecting the
consequences of such disharmony in her sense of self, Janis'
relationships were shifting, intense, dramatic, unstable,
exploitative, and often destructive to both her and her lovers.
Thus, these descriptions of Janis are disturbingly familiar to
clinicians who work with patients struggling with identity
problems.

Sex, Drugs And Rock And Roll: Living In The Here And

Now

Janis' biographers describe her rampant impulsivity. Friedman's Janis is puzzled by people who "could still maintain some order to their souls."

> For herself, there were only extremes; a world of primitive, unbridled impulses; that, or a realm to police her. She simply could not contain herself without the most rigid of impositions, or so she felt (Friedman 1973, 58).

In 1965, early in her career before fame swept her away, Janis returned home and tried to insert herself back into the tame, conventional community of Port Arthur. By returning to a conventional life, to a local college, dressing conservatively and attending social activities, Janis hoped the constraints of life in Port Arthur would help her gain self control. Friedman believes she was willing to adhere to the norms of Port Arthur because she was petrified of her vulnerability to drugs and frightened of the effects *of* "speed", with its tendency to heighten her awareness of her inner pain. She was terribly anxious then because self-control was such an alien concept to her.

Predictably, Janis found no relief in Port Arthur. While the feelings of dread and inner desolation of those in the dead zone are often eased by structure and predictability in their daily lives, they are not eliminated. Impulses toward self-damaging actions are powerful and persistent. Sex and drugs are the two most common attractions in this case because they have very intense effects on the nervous system, effects in the present moment, immediate, and exciting. They can easily blunt one's awareness and experience of feelings originating from the dead zone.

In Janis' case her impulsive urges were only temporarily blocked, and after a short period of denial, burst forth unchecked, even in environments with external constraints.

After a year in Port Arthur, Janis left and returned to the life of a performing artist, sex, drugs, and rock and roll.

Later she became widely known to have indiscriminate sex with as many men as she could (and at times with women). The love she sought was neither emotionally mature nor was it reciprocal. Rather her sexual liaisons were empty and unsatisfying, leaving Janis continually disappointed and eventually demoralized. Her incessant posturing about finding "a piece of talent" and getting laid was driven by impulses she readily allowed, in fact, could never contain, no matter what.

This failure of impulse control extended to drugs as well, a fact that is also widely documented. She was unable to resist alcohol, heroin, barbiturates and amphetamines, though they offered her only temporary relief while leading to her death.

Where's Everybody Going?

> There is no one here at all,
> sometimes not even me.
> I have no thoughts beyond despair,
> No dreams except of death.
> > From a poem by a patient living in the dead zone.

In the movie *The Rose*, loosely based on her last years, Janis' character falls to the ground outside a bar and cries out "Where's everybody going?" after her latest boyfriend leaves, fed up with her dramatic boozing and indiscriminate behavior. Here, in that agonizing wail for which Janis was so famous, an actress captured the poignant torment of the desolate, inner world, a world without images and representations of people, which left Janis fragile and helpless to stop the downward spiral.

In the light of clinical developments since her death, what is revealed by her need for constant, intense affects and activity is a need to stifle or suppress the dread that lurks just beneath the thin veneer of everyday living. In some indescribable way Janis must have been aware of her own dead zone, reflected as it was in the despair and unbearable sense of emptiness she

41

experienced in a life without meaning. She was not able to escape this ongoing existential nightmare through excitement and distraction, though she didn't stop trying until her death.

So Janis couldn't experience herself as a person, woman or partner. She was truly a lost soul with talent, faced with the impossibility of the need-fear dilemma in intimate relationships and who acted primarily on narcissistic needs and impulses. Her tumultuous life was filled with incessant commotion. The sense of herself as an ongoing, continuous, and enduring being was absent unless she was engaged in intense, on-the-edge activity. Aimless and lost, always seeking the thrill, the next intense experience to assuage the pain generated by eternal feelings of hopelessness and dread, she finally succumbed to the consequences of severe drug and alcohol abuse.

Janis functioned inconsistently, had no center, and no focus. Her personal attachments were followed by disregard or hostility. She adopted one, then another dramatic or symbolic identity (victim, tough guy, sex queen, party animal, anti-establishment heroine, rock star and so on). None of these identities gave her what she needed: a stable, cohesive sense of herself with the capacity to self-soothe and quiet her inner discord. Reflecting the consequences of this inner discord, her relationships were shifting, intense, dramatic, unstable, and exploitative, or mutually destructive.

Janis: After All

Janis' experiences in that nightmare are no surprise to clinicians who work with the *dramatic, emotional, and empty* patient. Based on our current clinical understanding of psychology and personality, we are now able to answer questions that many have asked.

1. What was the matter with her? Why was her life such a chaotic affair?

Based on the information we have gathered for this book from the observations of her biographers, the portrayal of her in films and recorded personal interviews with her, what we have found after all these years may be expressed by pointing to characteristic features of Janis' personality:

- a clear pattern of instability in interpersonal relationships;
- an unstable and vague self-image and identity;
- shifting and unpredictable moods;
- poor control of impulses and emotions beginning in early adulthood and evident in a variety of contexts.
- a pervasive feeling of emptiness/deadness

This description happens to be consistent with a well researched, conceptually and empirically established psychiatric diagnosis of *Borderline Personality Disorder* as defined by the *Diagnostic and Statistical Manual of the American Psychiatric Association* (DSM-IV, see appendix 1) and by the work of such brilliant clinicians, Otto Kernberg, John Gunderson, Gerald Adler, Roy Grinker, Robert Knight, and many other psychoanalytic investigators who have described the varied characteristics of these personalities over many decades.

Thus, in modern clinical terms, the response to the first question is that she was increasingly incapacitated by a personality disorder that was little known or understood at that time. Her chaotic life may now be understood as derived from that disorder. In their panic to escape inner feelings of tension and dread, most borderline personality types like Janis' dramatic example tend to cut a wide life path filled with debris. (There are also *isolative* types). Many of the people we read about in the daily news and about whom we wonder, "How could they do that?" or "What a stupid thing to do?" or "Why would anyone act that way?" may well be struggling with borderline disorders. We are only now beginning to recognize such behaviors as revealing disorder beneath the surface. It is very possible that many of the violent and destructive interpersonal conflicts between spouses or partners, many drug and alcohol related incidents, auto accidents, and many impulsive acts of sexual promiscuity, verbal assault and self-destructive behavior that fill the newspapers everyday are associated with people suffering from various borderline personality disorders.

2. How did she die? Did she kill herself?

We obviously can never know for certain. At that time, Thomas T. Noguchi, M.D., chief medical examiner for the county of Los Angeles found that Janis died of an accidental overdose of heroin, though the presence of alcohol in her blood was also noted. Test results for other drugs were negative, and the medical examiner found no evidence of violence or foul play. The possibility of suicide was considered and apparently discarded.

As with many public figures who died under unusual circumstances, her death began great speculation as to why and how she died. Some are patently absurd and we will not take up space to discuss them, i.e., that she was killed by the CIA, or by drug lords. But the question remains as to how she died. Was it suicide? Was it really an *accidental* drug overdose?

Both Friedman in *Buried Alive* and Laura Joplin in *Love Janis* were insistent that Janis did not commit suicide, not consciously. They point to the greater likelihood of a drug interaction between the heroin and alcohol. The possibility of a dose of heroin too pure for her body, or of an actual overdose is pondered by Friedman. On this line, then, despite her lifelong struggle with despair, Janis had shown no signs of suicidal tendencies immediately prior to her death. In fact, she was excited and ready to record a new song, *Buried Alive in the Blues,* according to Friedman. None of her actions in the 24 hours preceding her death were unusual. The most reasonable explanation for the immediate cause of death seems to be as these two biographers and the Chief Medical Examiner have suggested.

If Janis did not kill herself, but instead was simply another unlucky drug user, then the question as to why did she take drugs is pertinent, though already described: she did it to help her manage a despair and unbearable inner tension which was laying waste to her emotional life. Her death should not be considered a consciously intentional suicide by any means. Rather it came as a consequence of engaging in behaviors aimed at escaping the barrenness of life in the dead zone.

3. How was she different if at all from the many other public figures who died prematurely by their own hand?

It is now safe to assert that there are other public figures who suffered then as others do now, with one or another borderline condition. Many clinicians are certain enough that they cite the examples of Zelda Fitzgerald and Marilyn Monroe. Monroe was treated for years by the well-known and highly regarded psychoanalyst, Ralph Greenson. Monroe's biographers record chronic behaviors that are consistent with what we know today to be borderline conditions. In her case, like Janis', clinical psychiatry had not yet framed the outlines of the condition.

But by and large, public figures like James Forrestal, Ernest Hemingway, Sylvia Plath, Anne Sexton, Bruno Bettleheim, and more recently Vince Foster and Kurt Cobain appear **not** to have been suffering from a borderline condition. Rather they appear to have been suffering from one or another form of undiagnosed depression. Each clearly intended to kill themselves. The suspicion now runs deep among clinicians that Elvis Presley, John Belushi and River Phoenix may also have been caught in the psychological trap of dependence on drugs and may or may not have been depressed. They do not appear to have been borderline disorders.

What is clear is that Janis was not like most public figures who die by their own hand. Many borderlines, unlike Janis, die indirectly as a consequence of a borderline condition, and are typically not able to become very public figures. Generally, a moderate to severe borderline condition makes it difficult for someone to achieve and maintain public recognition except by negative behaviors and the subsequent fallout.

4. What difference does this information make?

This newer understanding of Janis' borderline condition can alert us to its symptoms and its recognizable consequences.

Reading her biographies and watching the few films of her performances, one is moved by Janis' powerhouse talent, the sadness one easily senses behind her wisecracking humor and the torment in her singing. Impulse-ridden, wracked by a wretched hunger for human attachments and the inability to be satisfied or soothed by them, lacking any inner sense of being, unable to truly connect with anyone, Janis' agony poured out in that wailing, flailing, tormented voice. We are convinced that part of her hold on audiences had to do with the way the pain in her voice touched some of the existential despair in all of us.

Chapter Four: Reflections On Destiny—Therapy with Janis

"Oh Lord won't you buy me a Mercedes-Benz"

The richness and complexity of Janis Joplin's personality are not encompassed by her emotional disturbances. She was not simply the sum of the parts of the psychopathology described here. Her biographers uniformly describe a vibrant, exciting, instinct-driven, let-it-all-hang-out girl-woman who was also brash, trashy, generous, compassionate, sexual, very intelligent, sensitive and much more. Just how these and other salient characteristics combined with her conflicts to create the original that she proved to be is beyond our comprehension.

Her sexual liaisons were a consuming preoccupation (second only to heroin and alcohol). They included dozens of men and women of all types including public figures such as Kris Kristofferson (who wrote her biggest hit, "Me and Bobby McGee"), Joe Namath, Jimi Hendrix, and Jim Morrison to name a few. For a long time she continued a public relationship with the Hell's Angels, inviting them to her concerts and even singing at one of their parties before finally becoming disillusioned. She turned away, strained, or undermined every good, potentially stable relationship with lovers, friends, and relatives through her drug and alcohol use, her sexual promiscuity and her often extreme, dramatic behavior. At the same time her friends and colleagues seemed quite tolerant of her behavior, as though they sensed her to be a tormented, still innocent girl who was more deserving of empathy than condemnation.

This complicated personality, with all its contradictions and inner agonies, proved to be a powerhouse of energy who became a new, original song stylist and interpreter of folk, blues, jazz, and country music. She joined with her audiences emotionally and sometimes, especially in her last year or two, openly encouraged her concert audiences to sing, dance and make love, much to the consternation of the security guards. Her audiences loved her and expected her to be irreverent, talking directly to them, urging them to "get it on" between and even during songs about sex and life (See the captivating pair of photographs by Bill Higgins in the Myra Friedman book, portraying someone from the audience reaching up on-stage to touch Janis' hand).

Janis would take a swing at anyone who insulted her or behaved threateningly, and was "punched out" herself on occasion. Irony and tragedy are to be found in her life as well as in Morrison's. Each died at a time when the condition with which they struggled was being actively investigated and articulated.

In fact as early as 1967, Otto Kernberg diagnosed what he labeled "borderline personality organizations." By the early to mid-seventies, clinical research on the diagnosis and treatment of these disorders was well under way and yielding impressive results. Kernberg was developing a modification of psychoanalysis called "expressive psychotherapy," and by 1974 clinical communities were progressing rapidly in their capabilities to treat borderline patients. One cannot help but wonder then what might have been, for example, had Janis been treated by Dr. Kernberg at Cornell University or Dr. Gunderson at Harvard University, who was also exploring borderline conditions.

Janis is known to have seen a mental health professional on two or three occasions. She asked to be admitted to a psychiatric hospital in 1965, telling them she felt "crazy." At that time she had been using amphetamines (uppers, which would tend to intensify her inner turmoil, while causing a serious deterioration in her mental functioning). According to Friedman's account, the hospital refused to admit her because she was perceived to be malingering, looking for a place to sleep.

In an earlier episode in Texas, she saw a clinical social worker because she was concerned about her drug use and her emerging need to control herself. Apparently deciding that her level of pathology was significant, the clinician who saw her that day described Janis as "diffused"—a clear symptom of an unstable personality. He warned her about the attendant costs to her mental health posed by the pressures of performing. However, aside from the caution he urged her to exercise, and lacking any conceptual framework which might permit a more insightful analysis of her condition, he could not offer her an effective treatment.

We are intrigued by the possibilities as to how her fate might have been different had she been accurately evaluated and effectively treated. After researching his life, it is our sense of Jim Morrison that he would have been a more difficult candidate for psychotherapy than Janis. It is simply difficult to imagine him seeking help. He so completely engaged his intellect in the pursuit of the "dark side," so assuredly saw the problems of his life as emanating from outside himself, and was so hostile to convention that he simply would have engaged in verbal warfare with the therapist. Although his lifelong sadism, narcissism, and hostility are personality traits associated with poor outcome in psychotherapy, we think nevertheless he would have been a challenging and interesting patient.

We believe that the emerging models of borderline conditions available to therapists have greatly enhanced their success with such patients. In this chapter, we offer an informed look at what a psychotherapeutic session with either Janis or Jim might have been like (had either decided to enter into that process). Could they have been helped? Or would they have frustrated the process as so many like them have?

Imagine if you will, a course of psychotherapy as we have constructed it for Janis, and later Jim, based on our sense of them from what others have written and on a modern clinical understanding of the various borderline conditions. Using my own experiences with these kinds of patients, I (GAF) present portions of five sessions, a first, eleventh, twelfth, twentieth and twenty-eighth with Janis, to illustrate how the process might have evolved with each of them. I use my own theoretical framework and clinical style, attempting to portray them in a manner consistent with their recorded dialogue, individual idiosyncracies and the record of their life experiences, biographies, movies, and documents each wrote. I will begin with Janis.

Janis is sent by her friends and associates who are worried about her drug and alcohol abuse, fluctuating emotional states, and agitated state of mind. She has agreed to see a clinician because her drug abuse concerns her too now, as it did from time to time . She has also been very depressed and as always, very lonely.

Session 1.

It is late September of 1970, one week after twenty-seven year old Jimi Hendrix died by choking in circumstances involving drug use (Janis died two weeks later at age 27. Jim Morrison nine months later—age 27). She is dressed in her uniquely Janis clothes designed by Linda Gravenites (Friedman 1973, 87-88), including love beads, bracelets and sandals. She is overweight, has acne on her face, and looks exhausted. There is something childlike about her despite her well known use of rough language and the dramatic way she presents herself.

GAF: Please come in.
(We shake hands. Her hand feels firm but tense; not unusual for a first visit to a therapist. I note her hip clothes and her attempt to appear casual and easy. Further, not being a rock fan at that time, I had no knowledge of Janis Joplin and Jim Morrison. However, we can assume she would have expected me to have been aware of her popularity and her music. Nervously she looks around, smiling, and giggling slightly. She sits down and looks amusingly at my office

*arrangement. I explain briefly
how the therapy process works.
Then we begin.)*
Why do you think you need to
see me?

Janis: Well I'm not sure doc, my
friends think I need some help.
*(A brief sample of her famous
cackle laugh, then sadly)* And I
feel really down a lot. *(Another
pause, then a quick change of
mood.)* By the way doc, who
does your decorating?

GAF: How do you mean? *(With raised
eyebrows.)*

Janis: Well, it's a bit dull in here. You
could use a lot more color and
some curtains to start with.

GAF: Really?
*While Janis was widely known
to be brash, impulsive, and
dramatic, it is very clear from
our research that these features
of her personality are consistent
with someone afflicted with an
hysterical type of borderline
disorder, someone who, for
example, tends to become
"familiar" with strangers
quickly.)*

Janis: Yeah, you need something to
make it real, things here and

there, to . . . like make it alive, man. I mean, you know, more groovy. *(Her emotional state changes again and after a long pause and some more looking around, the therapist's silence moves her back to subject at hand.)* I don't know why . . . don't know why I do some of the things I do. I'm trying to have a good time . . . . It's just that I, you know . . . feel . . . I don't know . . . really bad most of the time. *(Janis stares out the window, her head moving slowly, despairingly from side to side. The skin on her face seems loose and sagging. Her body lay sprawled in the chair as if thrown there like a discarded coat.)*

GAF: Uh huh.

Janis: You know, like I've got all these people around, friends, chicks, and cats . . . and they're cool, but they're never really there when you need them. Especially the cats. They're all users. I get it on a lot but it doesn't last. *(More "cool" jargon followed by another moment of sadness, then another shift.)* So, do you like rock, blues, jazz, or what?

GAF: Why do you ask?

Janis: Oh just curious. *(She then recites a litany of complaints about uptight and boring people, society, prejudices, cats, chicks and the general unfairness of life. She is very animated and intense, very articulate and clearly well read. Yet at the same time, in her tone and choice of words, she has somehow managed to let me see her unrelenting anxiety__and agitation. Janis is apt to act overtly and become verbal, physical, or emotional rather than simply withdraw in order to contain her demons.)*
Well, what do you think?

GAF: Mmm. Why don't we just continue?

Janis: Yeah, but can you help me?

GAF: I don't know yet. Tell me more about yourself.

Janis: Yeah okay. I . . . it's hard man . . . I mean things seem, sometimes I feel like I can't . . . can't *(pensive, silent, then resumes)* I think sometimes it's just too much. Maybe Jimi had it right.

GAF: Jimi?

Janis: Yeah, Jimi Hendrix. They say

he choked to death last week. At least he went out famous. We made it for a while last year, he was right on, man. I'm getting fed up too . . . just tired of all the bullshit. And everybody thinks I use too much.

GAF: Uh huh. Do you?

Janis: I don't know. I can handle it. But I need it, man. I need it . . . . *(Again a desperate look, an imperceptible shudder from this tormented human being.)*

GAF: What do you use?

Janis: Heroin mostly. And downers.

GAF: Other drugs?

Janis: I tried speed but its not for me. And I don't do acid or grass anymore either.

GAF: How come?

Janis: I feel terrible on uppers, like weird and nervous. And grass makes me think too much. I saw a social worker in Texas once when I was trying to shake the uppers. He was helpful, but I still . . . I don't know.

GAF: Uh huh. How about alcohol?

Janis: Yeah . . . alcohol, too. It helps.

GAF: Helps?

Janis: You know, it just helps.

GAF: Helps what?

Janis: I don't know, it just helps. Jesus. *(After a short silence)* Well? *(Looking worried now)* Aren't you gonna say something? What do you want me to say? I just need it. I just need it. All I want is a little peace, *(Her words become almost inaudible as she pensively looks out of the window. Janis slumps back, frowns at me and throws her boa on the floor. Even in this moment of reflection she seems to be sitting too still like a coiled spring on the verge of expansion.)* . . . just a little fucking peace.

GAF: Peace?

Janis: Yeah, a little peace. (*Again frowning and impatient.*)

GAF: Peace from what?

Janis: I don't know, I'm always . . . I don't know. I don't know, it just never stops. I'm on edge all the time.

GAF: What never stops?

Janis: The bullshit, the goddamn bullshit. I mean like it's hard man, it's just hard. Never quiet, never peaceful. Always, you know . . . like uneasy. It used to be more fun sometimes, but now it's just . . . I don't know, man . . . it's all fucked up. Nothing feels good anymore. I don't know, I think I'm going crazy. Can't get to feeling really groovy, not ever. I'm just . . always uneasy. And just don't lecture me about drugs, I know what I'm doing and I'm careful.

GAF: Uneasy?

Janis: Yeah, uneasy. It's always the same no matter what. I'm really down most of the time. *(long silence)* It's hopeless. I don't know . . . .

GAF: *(Silence)*

Janis: *(stares)* Yeah. It's like hopeless, man, just hopeless, and . . . lonely, like nothing . . . like something's missing. Yeah, like I'm bored, really bored, and, oh Fuck. So is it hopeless? *(nervous laugh)*. What can I do about it? *(Now, Janis is trying to get away from her hopeless mood. She brightens up, recovers from the slumped position, and resumes eye contact with me.)*

GAF: Well, we'll try and find out.

Janis: Okay. What else do you want to know?

GAF: What else would you like to tell me?

Janis: Are you ever going to answer a question? Well let's see, I was born dirt poor in a small, cold, shack. *(smiles jokingly, now, with her eyes wide open while she leans forward in the seat.)* Okay, I'm from Port Arthur, Texas. I have one sister and one brother. My father is a great guy, a secret intellectual. My mother is a lot of things, musical, smart, a great teacher.

GAF: Uh huh.

Janis: I've got a new album out. Working on a groovy new one, "Buried Alive in the Blues." *(There's a long silence. Of course this is an ironic choice of titles considering her emotional state.)* Do you have many VIP patients?

GAF: What makes you ask? *(Considering Janis' risk for suicide, I wonder about her VIP question and whether it is connected with her previous comment about Jimi Hendrix.)*

Janis: Oh, no reason, just curious.

GAF: You mentioned Jimi Hendrix?

Janis: Yeah. He was cool man. He did some great things and then checked out at his peak. That's how he'll be remembered.

GAF: Is that how you're feeling?

Janis: Naw, just thinking about it. Besides, Jimi stole the show for this year. But I can't stand much more of this shit. I just can't stand it. I mean, everything feels like shit . . . can't ever just . . . *(She begins to look depressed and becomes agitated. After a brief silence, she looks up and, with the wave of her hand, tries to shake off the question but quickly begins to look depressed and becomes mildly agitated.)* So what now? What do I do now?

GAF: You're feeling like shit now?

60

Janis: Yeah, so what? You fucking shrinks are all alike, never answer a question straight. *(Now becoming more irritated, rapidly twiddling her fingers).*

GAF: Is this what you mean by being on edge? *(Together with the sudden shifts in emotion, her quickness to anger, and to become incensed with me—a stranger, afterall, whose help she is seeking, I now suspect the presence of serious pathology.)*

Janis: *(Just looks at me, now calmly, as if my observation relieved some of the tension).* Yeah . . . I guess so . . . yeah. *(Mood shifts and she smiles wanly.)*

Janis: *(Looking out window, slowly becoming sad again and wistful. After a long while).* So what's the matter with me anyway?

GAF: How do you mean?

Janis: You've had other patients like me?

GAF: Yes, but what is it like for you?

Janis: Uh . . . I don't know,
Never thought about it
before.

GAF: Uh Huh.

Janis: Guess it's the way I've
always been. Even
when I'm having a
blast, it's like . . .
always there.

GAF: Even when you're having a blast?

Janis: Yeah, all the time. It
never fucking stops. I
get that way even on
stage sometimes when
things slow down. It's
strange. That I never
thought much about it
before. It's really
fucking awful. *(Another
long pause, and her
face takes on a look of
newfound puzzlement,
with raised eyebrows
and wrinkled forehead.)*
Maybe Jimi felt like
this, too.

GAF: *(I try to help Janis*

clarify her behavior patterns.) Are you aware of wanting to drink when you're having those awful feelings? Or take drugs?

Janis: Yeah, like after a show I look for a party cause I can't stand to just go home and do nothing. It's too . . . lonely . . . or empty . . . or something. So I wanna have a good time, find a cat I can ball, you know, have a blast. But you're right, I always feel kinda . . . it's a bummer man, a real bummer.

GAF: Uh huh.

Janis: You know, the same thing happens with drugs. It's like . . . the same thing man, it's all the same fucking thing. It's really bad . . . feeling so lonely, I mean. All the time, man, all the time and . . . oh, man. *(She stares out window, tears well up)*

GAF: *(Janis is working well*

63

on her own. Comments from me are unnecessary at this point as they might interfere with her mood and associations. So I acknowledge her feelings with a neutral response which just restates her words and then I remain silent) Mmmm. You mean you party, have sex, and do drugs when you're feeling like shit or on edge?

Janis: Yeah, that's right. All I want is some peace from this . . . this fucking whatever it is! Jesus Christ! . . . . I'm so tired, so tired. *(Another long silence)* I can't believe this.

GAF: Believe what?

Janis: That this is happening, like I'm all fucked up. Why do I always feel so bad? Like I don't belong anywhere. If it doesn't get better than this then the hell with it. It's just too lonely all the time, no matter what

I do. *(Interestingly one of her songs is A Woman Left Lonely)* And what am I doing here with a shrink, a goddamn shrink, like I'm a fucking schizo? I don't need this shit. *(Janis stares angrily at the floor and once again discards the boa. She slowly looks up at me as if expecting an answer to her comments.)*

GAF: (Silence)

Janis: How come you just sit there? Don't you have anything to say? What do you think? Jesus. I'm here trying to get my fucking head together and you're just sitting there. *(Eyebrows arching angrily and on the edge of the seat leaning toward me.)*

GAF: If you remember, we discussed at the beginning of the session how this therapy works. I'll be listening to you carefully and trying to understand what you are telling me. I'll offer you my thoughts when I think they might be helpful to you.

Janis: Yeah, *(Janis caves in the face of this mild reminder)* sorry. I remember. Okay. It's really strange, though. I've always lived my life full tilt . . . like the name of my band. Some artists separate their private from their professional lives, but I never have. I go all out, no limits. Some of my friends think I'll try anything. I'm out for fun and I've done it all and do it all. So why am I so very miserable most of the time? It's awful, just awful. I've had a very successful year on stage, I have a funky house, clothes, I must've balled fifty cats, *(typical Janis Joplin bravado)* had tons of booze and drugs, and I still feel like shit all the time, this boredom, this emptiness. Why's this happening to me, huh doc?

GAF: Maybe we can figure it out together.

Janis: Yeah . . . Okay. It's just that I get so lonely. And I'm driven. I don't know why I do things.

GAF: Do things?

Janis: Yeah, I get groovin and anything goes. People tell me I have a filthy mouth and no sense of moderation. I guess I'm an extremist. *(Silence)* I meet all kinds of people in my work, all the rock artists and show business types. *(Stares off vaguely)* You really think we can do something about this? Really? *(Without waiting for response, Janis settles down and moves on to another subject.)* So, do you like rock, or jazz, or blues? I hope you're not too boring.

GAF: How do you mean?

Janis: Well, if we're going to work together . . . I was just curious.

This first session went very well. Janis was more emotionally temperate than she would be in subsequent sessions. She learned for the first time to try to comprehend her inner state of feeling and that there might be a way of understanding it. And she seems to have become somewhat comfortable with me, joking and poking fun, and at the end, deciding to continue. Compared to therapists of the sixties, I possess a clinical framework for conceptualizing and treating her condition, a significant advantage. After only one session, I begin to suspect that her "boredom" and "uneasiness" and "loneliness" are common feelings expressed by those experiencing the dead zone—one descriptive label given by patients suffering from this type of borderline condition. But further assessment is needed.

Sessions 2 through 9

Through more history taking, I expand on the material gathered in the first session, attempting to clarify Janis' experiences of emptiness and impulsivity. She takes the therapist to task again for his boring taste in decor while she repeatedly complains about her bad luck with men, providing a detailed description of her latest relationship with Seth Morgan. She continues to express the hope for a quick, magical cure for her feelings of despair, leaving the session hopeful but anxious. We have agreed to meet three times each week.

Indirectly seeking again to learn whether I have heard of her, she talks about the rock scene she knows so well and her latest performance. Together we examine her continual use of drugs and alcohol.

Session 10.

Janis doesn't show, but by now I am becoming more certain that she is suffering from a borderline syndrome.

Session 11.

Janis arrives dressed more conservatively than in the first few sessions, her hair styled in a more restrained fashion, her mood upbeat. Appreciative of my work with her , she seems to be genuinely interested in continuing her therapy. She makes, however, no mention of missing the previously scheduled hour.

Janis: *Immediately on entering)* Feeling good today, Doc. But you were right last session about me and smack. I gotta stop. Went and used minutes after I left your office. Don't even know why. Just wanted some. *(Janis is puzzled, perhaps for the first time, consciously reflecting on her drug abuse. We had discussed her loneliness and how she seemed always to be attracted to unstable men or drove stable men away. We then tied her actions to her need for drugs and she seemed to "get it," although it's uncertain just what she "got." She looks brighter than last time and her eyes flash playfulness and exuberance as she slides into the leather recliner, putting her legs over one arm and pulling the lever to open the leg rest.)*

GAF: Right after you left my office? Do you remember how you were feeling?

Janis: Well, I was headed for a recording session. Remember, I told you about it? It's going to be FAN-tastic. And I told you before that my last one is doing great. *(Janis is still searching for ways to find out what I might think of her work.)* And I needed something. I know everyone is down on me for using. And Uncle Albert *(*Albert Grossman, her manager) isn't cool about it either. He gets like, all crazy when he thinks his stars are using. *(Notice how she lets me know about her star status. Most borderline patients have strong narcissistic* *tendencies.)*

GAF: You needed something?

Janis: Yeah, you know, like just needed to, uh, you know, just uhh, . . . so what? Jesus. You're always at it. I can't stand it. You've always got to question everything. Can't you just take it for what it is? *(Janis is quite irritated with me. She would like to go on narrating her story and having my full attention. When I raise questions she is reminded of why she is there, and it spoils her fantasies of impressing me.)* Haven't you ever read Ferlinghetti or Kerouac or anything but those goddamn textbooks? Does everything have to be Freudian? I told you that I can handle it. I just wanted to let you know that you were right about me using after our sessions. Can't you just give me a little credit for something?

What is it with you?

GAF: Well, you say you needed something right after you left my office, and I wondered about how you were feeling then. I wondered if it's perhaps hard for you to leave each time?

Janis: *(A long silence)* Yeah, so what? *(Becoming very quiet now and almost inaudible.)* Yeah, I do feel like that, uh . . . I don't want to go, like I want to stay longer. *(Once again Janis seems to shrink in size and appears lost in the chair. I find it hard to avoid thinking of her as a sad and scared little girl.)*

GAF: So when you do walk out the door, what are you feeling?

Janis: Uh . . . I guess it's uh, it's just . . . it's like shit, man, like shit. Fucking lousy, empty. . . . *(Janis begins to get in touch with the feeling.)*

GAF: Empty, is that the feeling we've been talking about?

Janis: Yeah, I guess so, I guess so, it's really hard to describe.

GAF: So when you're here you feel better and when you leave here you feel alone and empty?

Janis: Yeah. I can't stand it, it's like a goddamn nightmare and you're the only one who can stop it, here in your office. And there I am, leaving. Everything ends until the next session. So I go looking for friends and some smack and try to keep going till the next session. Like there's nothing else but here. Everything seems so goddamn unimportant, so unreal. I just want to get by until I'm back here. Can't you do something? What is this, why am I like this? Why me? Jesus. (*Tears well up again and it's easy to see that she's*

73

angry. She frowns and become agitated.)

GAF: So you need drugs to take away the uneasy feelings . . . except that they take away all your feelings?

Janis: Right on. And you, you're hard, man. You stick to the time like you don't care. *(Janis is now escalating emotionally and mocks me)* We have to stop now, we have to stop now. . . like your time is so fucking important. Well my time is, too, man. I have a tight schedule just as important as your is, you think you're so goddamn cool. So smart, like you know it all. Well, fuck you man, just fuck off with all your questions. *(Now Janis is in a full blown outburst, staring at me, the expression on her face filled with rage)* I don't need this, fuck this, what do you want from me anyway? Asshole. Fuck you.

74

Fuck you!

GAF: You'd prefer it if I didn't follow the rules with you, made an exception? *(I remain unruffled, silently communicating to her that I can withstand her anger, and that I will resolutely seek to determine what it all means.)*

Janis: *(Screaming now)* I don't care what the fuck you do. You're just in this for the money like everybody else. *(After standing up and pacing around the room she hurls another "fuck you" and "fucking asshole", then leaves, slamming the door and cursing as she charges down the corridor.)*

This is a good example of the complexity of working with this kind of patient. Janis clearly was experiencing the intense and dreadful feeling of abandonment, the central feeling of the dead zone, each time our sessions ended.

It is typical for borderline personalities to form quick, intense attachments to people and become very dependent and demanding. It is also common for many of them to have unpredictable outbursts for no apparent reason (because of what is going on internally). She became enraged when I maintained the boundaries of the therapy by staying on schedule because she felt entitled to special treatment, and because she felt her ever present emptiness and despair upon separating from the therapist. Yet any violation of the strict boundaries of therapy would make her worse.

Her reaction was to seek escape, in this case by drug use. When I attempted to connect the feelings of abandonment with her use of drugs, she "got it" and felt understood for a moment, and thus more connected to me. But this only made leaving at the end of the hour that much more dreadful, and she exploded in rage. Considering that this is the first time Janis has been given any hope of bringing her sense of inner despair under control, one is reminded of the axiom some have applied to the treatment of borderline patients: "no good deed will go unpunished."

Session 12.

Janis arrives on time, calm and matter of fact. Her weight is up and her eyes are ringed and bloodshot. She raises the incident of the previous hour and her stormy exit.

Janis: So what's up? I suppose
         you want to talk about
         last time. You always
         want to understaaand
         everything. Maybe
         some things are just
         what they are. Maybe
         this is just intellectual
         masturbation.   Maybe
         none of this means
         anything. *(Janis's
         sarcasm betrays the
         anger still there).*

GAF: It would help if we could
       sort out what happened last

time.

Janis: I don't know, I just felt pissed off. *(Drawn and demoralized, she lowers her head, gazing only at the floor. She has clearly been having a hard time.)*

GAF: You seemed all right until we began talking about how dreadful you feel at the end of each session. Could it be that you've been angry about always having to leave, about always feeling that way, and finally let go of the feeling?

Janis: I guess I do get pissed off after I leave here, even if I liked what we talked about. *(Janis leans forward, her elbows on her knees, chin cupped in palm of her hand, and eyes looking up with eyebrows raised. She is sad, puzzled and perhaps a little embarrassed.)*

GAF: Perhaps that's why you

missed the session before last? *(I'm certain of what happened now and it will help Janis to know that I know.)*

Janis: What do you mean?

GAF: Maybe you stayed away to protect me from your wrath, from your anger at having to leave? *(I say this in a bit of a whisper for effect.)*

Janis: Goddamn. *(Smiling sheepishly)* You know about that. How do you know about that? I was so fucking pissed, I could've punched your face in. So I didn't come.

GAF: You were being considerate. You wanted to be sure you wouldn't injure me.

Janis: Yeah *(still smiling)* daddy, that's right. *Janis softens, sits back in the chair and moves on. The change in her mood is striking. She is no longer appears grim and fatigued. Instead a smile breaks out, and her tone is upbeat and playful.)* So, what shall we talk about today? Want to hear about my sex life? *(Janis is teasing me and bragging at the same time).*

GAF: Silence. *A patient like Janis will fill our sessions with grist for the mill, material for the therapeutic process. All I have to do is wait.)*

Janis: Well? (Teasing) What's the matter, doc, don't you like sex? I've balled all kinds of cats man, and chicks, too. Can't seem to get enough. I thought you were Freudian? It's all about sex isn't it? I mean, everybody's lookin to get laid. I'm just very good at it. But I never get enough. Always lookin'. Are you gettin enough, doc? Are you like me—never enough? *(Janis thinks she's on safer ground with sex, and knows her way around 'the scene'.)*

GAF: Enough?

Janis: Yeah, enough. I get laid all the time, and I'm always looking for new . . . talent. And I still want more action. It doesn't last long after so have to keep lookin'.

GAF: Mmm. Well, you make it sound like you have a voracious sexual appetite. But how is it that you're still wanting if you're getting laid all the time? *(I'm asking her to confront a contradiction here—she gets lots of sex but it doesn't last her very long. It appears that she is driven by the prospect of obtaining sexual gratification while she freely concedes that she is insatiable . I give no consideration to the idea that she is just a "very sexual person" as some of my patients have insisted. It seems clear enough from her accounts that sex is being used here like so*

many other things—
food, alcohol, work,
physicality to name a
few—as a means of
escaping   inner
confusion or conflict.)

Janis: I don't know, I'm just
after it all the time.
What's the difference?
Are you going to tell me
that sex is bad? Am I
supposed to be virginal
and a good little girl?
Come on, doc, are you
really that straight? I
want it all the time and
that's just the way it is.
Take love where you
find it. It may not be
here tomorrow. *(These*
lines, of course are
drawn from the music
she wrote.)

GAF: Is that the same reason
you're after drugs and
alcohol?

Janis: I guess so. *(Puzzled*
once again, Janis looks
at me wondering where
I'm headed with this
line of questions.)

GAF: Maybe there's more to it.

Janis: What do you mean? Sex is sex and I'm not repressed about it. The country is so uptight about sex, but I'm not buying into that crap. I'm not buying into the white house with the picket fence and all the girls are virgins crap. It's phony and hypocritical, and I have to tell it like it is. (R*eacting self-righteously*) So what do you mean there's more to it? (*Acting as if she were annoyed once again*)

GAF: There's sex and there's driven sex. You make it sound as though you're driven.

Janis: Well, a little maybe, I guess so. So what? It's all the same anyway man, all the same shit. How else do you expect it to be? What else is there? It's that or be lonely all the fucking time. (*Long silence. She may be feeling that I'm raining on her parade again, taking away self-*

82

*perspectives that were
of some comfort to her.)*

GAF: What about love,
sharing experiences,
affection, friendship,
feeling connected?
What you describe as
sex doesn't seem to
have much
connectedness. Only the
physical.

Janis: Well, yeah, maybe.
(Wistfully) But I did
connect with a few guys
and some other people.

GAF: If I recall our
discussions, you always
pick troublesome men
or behave so as to cause
problems for any
serious, straight
relationship.
Do I have that right?
*(Janis let's me proceed.
She is curious about
where I'm going.)*

Janis: Yeah, I guess so. I
always seem to be too
much—too much my
own person and they
can't handle that.
Besides, the straight
ones are usually boring.

83

(The problem she is describing expressed in clinical terms is that, for Janis, relationships without conflict are not intense enough to suppress the feelings from the dead zone. What is significant here is Janis's tendency to dismiss her own behaviors as having anything to do with her problems. This is a good example of her narcissistic side, again common in borderline patients).

GAF: Could it be that you're driven about sex for the same reasons that you are driven to take drugs and alcohol?

Janis: You mean the emptiness, the dead feeling?

GAF: Yes. You said it never stops.

Janis: *(A long pause after which she slowly shakes her head from side to side, then quietly)* Oh man . . . sometimes I don't care who it is, only that they're there and ready. It's the loneliness, I can't stand the loneliness. It's too hard and I get bored too and . . . uh . . . I get unbearably tense, yeah! (*Another long silence*) So that's it, isn't it? Like booze and drugs, I use sex to deal with it— the fucking emptiness? You're right, I dread it, I'll do anything. Anything. Anything. (*Looking very upset now.*) I mean. . . doc, like sometimes I don't even feel alive, feel real. Like there's no me, no nothing! Like something's missing.

GAF: Uh huh. Those feelings are partly responsible for your tensions and for your need to behave in extremes. It seems that it takes intense stimulation and excitement to help block those feelings.

Janis: Sex and drugs.

GAF: Yes. (*It will take awhile and many reminders*

before Janis will be able to remember this sex and drugs connection in her daily life. Only then will we be able to find ways to help.)

Janis: *(Now slumped in the chair, Janis is both pensive and sad. She looks quite small and fragile. The tough, wisecracking, modern day Bessie Smith of earlier sessions is temporarily subdued. My clarifying once again the relationship between her behavior and the dead zone is having some affect for the moment).* So what can I do? Am I hopeless?

GAF: We have to explore this together to see what we can do.

Janis: Okay. Let's do it. I can't stand the thought that it's going to be like this forever. I'd rather be dead. This is worse than dead. Everywhere I go I get down, sooner or later I get down. It's a goddamn bummer. All I want is to get my fucking head together, man, that's all. That's all. I gotta get my head together, gotta feel real.

GAF: Real?

Janis: Real, I don't know what I mean. It's just that I'm never sure I'm there, except maybe on stage . . . oh fuck. I don't know how to explain it, I just don't feel as though there's a me, as though I really exist. *(Janis looks very anxious and desperate.)*

During this session Janis identified and clarified the feelings she associated with the dead zone. She lacked the inner resources needed to soothe herself and to feel "real" and alive. Typical of borderline patients, she seemed unable to hold within herself the internalized images (representations) of the nurturing caretakers of childhood. This holding environment is a precondition necessary for all of us to regulate our emotional states, especially the experience of loneliness. Helping her to see more of her outrageous behaviors as symptoms of this devastating barrenness of her inner world gives her hope and direction.

Janis' futile efforts to find the internal resources to soothe herself and feel "real" left her, as always, despondent. Shortly after she began therapy, perhaps by the fifth or sixth session, she found that calling me to check in and hear my voice calmed her panicky feelings somewhat and improved her sense of being real (if I really existed then so did she). On her own she could not manage her crushing emptiness, the terrifying world of the dead zone. Her agonizing need for connectedness could not be gratified, because actual connecting would cause her to feel the threat of losing herself—her very existence—in the other person. On the other hand, her rage and hostility at the expectation of abandonment created an ever-changing, shifting internal state. Life was experienced as polarized: extreme attachments, extreme disappointments, extreme anger, and extreme anxieties. All of these needful feelings and internal demon images were regularly projected onto people involved with her, making stable relationships impossible.

Session 20.

Janis by this time (two months later at three times per week) is struggling with the vicissitudes of the therapeutic process. People will eventually act out their real conflicts, personality style, and tendencies in therapy, and Janis did so more quickly and more intensely than most.

Janis' intense "affect storms" of despair, anxiety, and outrage were difficult to contain in the first few months. She proved to be challenging, obstreperous, seductive, demanding, and infantile, as well as charming, warm, responsive, and entertaining. She struggled heroically to keep her psychic balance. I made every effort to follow her internal state of mind, help her identify the emptiness and disconnectedness behind her pain and bring her some relief. How difficult this is to accomplish, and the patience required to follow the endless twists and turns of her emotional roller coaster is again illustrated in the next session.

The previous two sessions were relatively calm for Janis as she reviewed her career and her love of singing, performing, and the limelight. In addition to shifting emotional states, she alternately gained and lost weight, and the severity of her acne waxed and waned. Her clothing varied too, with her appearing in a lengthy but simple hippie dress in one session, and during another in a heavily beaded, multicolored outfit set off by a feathered boa. These wildly fluctuating, highly ostentatious modes of dressing, along with chaotic behaviors, are symptomatic of the erratic functioning of the borderline personality. Clinicians often refer to that personality pattern as "stably unstable."

Janis arrived for this session in a cantankerous mood and somewhat disarrayed. She did not mention her phone call to me on the previous evening when she had felt frightened and wretched, and had vaguely threatened "not to put up with it" anymore.

Janis: *(She plops down, impatiently waiting for me to say something. Her arm has a pretty good size bandage on it and she is obviously unsettled as she moves about restlessly in the chair).* Well. Say something, you're just staring at me.

GAF: I see that you're not in a good mood.

Janis: *(Softens)* Naw, I'm just not in the mood for anything. I'm just tired, tired of people using me. Nobody really gives a damn about me, doc. Nobody really loves me. I'm sick of it. *(In a whiny, pleading voice now).* How come everybody leaves me? Everybody. The only people who love me are people who work for me, and then only 'cause I pay them.

GAF: What's happened since Monday? *(After our last meeting, two days ago, Janis left in an upbeat mood. While not surprised at her quick change in mood, I must try to determine what triggered it).*

Janis: Same old shit. Tried to get it on after a recording session Tuesday. We were out all night with some of the guys and I ended up kicking them out. All they did was drink my stuff and try to rob me blind. Fuckers. Jesus, I couldn't even get laid. They had grass, but I got wasted on booze and fell down the stairs in my own goddamn house. Look at this cut on my arm. I spent half the night in the fucking emergency room waiting for them to sew it up. Jesus. And a lot of my friends are gone— Nancy, Peggy, Kris . . . and Linda's mad at me, she hates drugs. I don't know, I'm just so tired, doc, just so tired.

GAF: Uh huh. This all happened after the recording session? Is that what you usually do afterward? Party all night?

Janis: Sure, getting it on, man. Have a ball, you know. Jesus, are you straight. But things are getting harder. It's really bad. I'm feeling bad all the time. I can't stand being down all the time I mean . . . fuck, nobody cares. If it keeps up I'm gonna end it, it's just too fucking much. (*Staring angrily at the floor.*)

GAF: Now wait. Help me understand this better. Walk me through the events, beginning with the recording session.

Janis: You know, it was a rehearsal session. We were getting ready for my new album and then had some fun with a few old songs and a few new ones that we're trying out. It was after one a.m. and I'm fucking exhausted. But a couple of the guys had their chicks hanging around and decided to get stoned. I can't stand that shit, gets my head all fucked up. Anyway, I invited everybody to my place, everybody. Four of the guys hopped in my car and we headed out. Then we get stopped by a cop who didn't like the looks of my car. *(Janis has a brightly painted psychedelic Porsche).* The cop spots my bottle, smells my breath and hands me a ticket. He won't let us move until one of the others gets behind the wheel. He starts giving me some jive shit about drinking and driving with this sneer on his face. So I jumped up to go after him and whack him with the bottle, but one of the guys pushed me down and sat on me till the cop got to his cruiser. He followed us all the way to my house. But then the party started and we had a blast until one of those obtuse fucking chicks came at me because she thought I was trying to get it on with her man. Big deal. I still don't know why she threw a fit. They had to pull me off her. I kicked her out and went down to get some smack. That's when I tripped on the stairs. I almost broke my neck and ended up in the emergency room with this cut. It took twelve stitches to sew my arm. When I got back everybody who's left is stoned out of their mind and the place is trashed. I kicked the whole bunch of them out on their collective asses.

GAF: How did you come to decide to invite

everyone to your
house?

Janis: What? (*Annoyed and
puzzled with wrinkled
brow.*)

GAF: I was wondering, how
after a long day, and at
one a.m., you felt like
partying when you were
already exhausted?

Janis: (*Mildly irritated*) I
don't know. What
difference does it
make? We were doing it
. . . getting it on . . .
getting down, man. Sex,
booze, drugs with my
friends. That's what we
do, man, that's making
the scene. We would
have gone to one of our
hangouts, too, if those
fuckers hadn't pulled
that shit.

GAF: Do you ever just go home
after a session?

Janis: No, man. That's when
we party. I can't believe
you, Jesus. Were you
ever young? Don't you
like having a good
time? Don't you like

fucking? Booze? Jeez. What do you do for fun, doc, or don't you like fun? Jeez. (*Janis is upset by my questions. She doesn't feel supported at this moment and turns away from me in the chair.*)

GAF: Then you'll party even if you're exhausted? (*I confront an incongruity: She needs to keep going, looking for excitement even when she's exhausted.*)

Janis: So? What are you getting at? I'm usually wound up after the sessions and after concerts. Could keep going all night. It's hard to stop. Everybody's feeling wasted and looking to get it on. I mean come on man, this is the scene, it's what's happening. Where the action is. How can you even ask that question? Time to go back to the books, doc. Don't you have a place in your philosophy, in your mind, that allows for

95

people getting it on? Jesus.

GAF: *(Silence)*

Janis: So? What . . . what are you getting at? What are you getting at anyway? *(Long silence with Janis staring at me.)* The emptiness, the hole, huh?

GAF: Well, is it possible? *(Janis needs to be reminded about the connection between her behavior and the dead zone. We have discussed it many times, yet she still must be directed to it. She acts up, cavorts, and goes on alcoholic binges while partying, and she is impulsive, impatient, and highly reactive to everything because she uses these behaviors to block the dread and confusion of feelings from the dead zone).*

Janis: Jeez . . . maybe. Everybody's out there, having a ball and I think that . . . maybe I always feel, really . . . apart from them. (*Janis is looking sad now and her "get it on" bravado dissolves as she becomes more reflective about the meaning of her behavior in this regard*). And I guess I didn't want to go home alone. I hate it. The nights are the worst. That's when I need smack the most . . . to numb out. You don't know, doc, you don't know how much I hate it . . . being alone, as if there's no one there. I can't even feel me there. Like I'm not, not . . . me. Like hollow, just an imaginary being. Maybe I'm a doppleganger, a ghost. Nothing solid, you can see right through me cause I'm not really here. I'm not really anywhere. I just can't stand it anymore. (*crying quietly, hand on her head tilted to one side.*)

GAF: All the excitement of people, drugs, sex, and

97

fighting—

Janis: Yeah . . . because I'm not alive. I'm not even dead. I'm just . . . not anything. *(Shaking her head, she stares at me a while, remembering many earlier sessions in which we had discussed the same problem).* I keep forgetting, don't I? What do I do . . . what, how can I get rid of it? Can't you tell me what to do?

GAF: It might help if you could keep it in the front of your mind. You might then recognize it when it starts to disrupt you and causes you to look for distractions. You could then say, Oh, there it is. I can't stand this. What can I do to keep it under control?

Janis: *(Looking up)* Yeah, then what? You've said before that it takes heavy action to block it, like sex, drugs—

GAF: If you can recognize it early then you might be

able to find new and better ways to contain it. We'll have to be very creative and experimental. And it would help if your life had more structure to it, more predictability—without cramping your freewheeling style too much. But we still need to keep working to understand your self-destructive behaviors, your tendencies to disrupt relationships and so on.

Janis: Yeah, I can be pretty impossible sometimes. But it really, really gets unbearable, doc. I hope you believe me. I'm not just making it up. I really need *(Teary-eyed and forlorn, Janis slumps in the chair looking both hopeful and scared. She begins to see her problem a little more clearly and wants to have hope despite her remaining skepticism. Her clothes have become a bit disheveled and she absentmindedly tries to straighten up.)*

GAF: I believe you. You were probably scared and feeling desperate like this when you called me yesterday, the day after the party, because you were alone with the emptiness.

Janis: Yeah . . . yeah . . . it was terrible after everyone left. That's why I called. I couldn't stand it, I, uh . . . I hate to admit it, but I felt much better the minute I heard your voice. I felt real again. It sounds stupid but it was like nothing seemed okay, until I knew that you were really there. I even have your cards all over. Like you're the only thing between me and nothing and I'm barely hanging on. It's crazy. What do I do, call you everytime I feel bad? I'd be on the phone all day. So, that's why I have people around all the time. I remember . . . we talked about this. *(Here again is yet another episode in her life that reveals the desolateness of her inner world. Not even her own physical existence can give her a sense of reality in the absence of internal "objects" as mentioned earlier.)*

GAF: Yes, you're in need of connecting with me and yet you're angry with me at the same time? (*A revealing contradiction of the borderline condition.)*

Janis: But I don't want you to be so important to me. It makes me angry, and I want to tell you to fuck off. It's scary because . . . because . . . I don't know. Don't want to be . . . to feel so helpless.

GAF: Could it be that you feel overwhelmed by how strong your feelings of need are, or perhaps that your needs and your rage would destroy me? (*Her exchanges with me here essentially describe the need, fear dilemma. Her overwhelming feelings of need are opposed by an equally overwhelming fear that the need will destroy the person or the needed person).*

Janis: That's right. If you're gone then I'd . . . like, like I'd have no one. It would be . . . I would be totally alone. Jesus. None of my friends make any difference anymore. They're really no help at all. I'd like to stay in your back pocket. I wouldn't be a bother. I'd just be able to see you and feel safe and real. But then I don't want to be like that—so helpless, so weak. It makes me hate everything, myself, you . . . . Jesus. (*Her torment raw and relentless, Janis begins to sob uncontrollably, obviously scared and utterly miserable.*)

GAF: (Another clarifying observation is useful

102

here, restating the connections between her inner states and her outer behavior). Maybe if we can understand it more fully, we can be more effective in helping you.

Janis: Yeah. *(Looking up, eyes red, nose running, she uses a facial tissue and calms down).* I can't see anyway out. The loneliness, it's unbearable. Worse than dead.

GAF: Yes. It appears that you're always feeling those dreadful feelings, the black hole. You feel them when you're alone, when you're with people in a not too stimulating situation, when you're done with a stage performance, when a relationship isn't intense enough, when you're too attached to someone, when you leave my office after a session, when anyone leaves you and when it's time to end the day. You feel it all the time and have as

far back as you can
remember.

Janis: *(Looking up sadly
contemplating my
summary, she then
finishes the description
of her behavior, clearly
demonstrating a fine
intelligence amidst the
anarchy of her life).*And
so I do anything to get
away from it. Sex, any
sex. Drugs, mostly
heroin because it numbs
me out, and alcohol
because it's easier to
use almost anywhere
and . . going all-out in
my performances on
stage. Getting the
audience all worked up
can numb me to my
goddamn misery . . .
and when everything
else fails I can act up or
instigate some kind of
disturbance to help out.
I'm impulsive, and
unpredictable, and
create all kinds of
trouble that turns
people off and fucks up
the chances of my
having a decent
relationship with
anybody. I guess that's

about it isn't it? My whole life is one big fucking diversion, right . . . just a hopeless attempt to escape from myself. Nothing. Nothing! (*Janis is almost screaming here.*)

GAF: It is a sad situation. But you've never been able to describe and it understand it until now.

Janis: Yeah, sure. So now I'll be better informed when I end it. Jesus, it's unbelievable. Maybe this is all a bunch of crap. Maybe I'm just fucked up, maybe it's too late. *(Janis is hoping I'll contradict her maybes. For most patients with the borderline syndrome, expressing ambivalence is typical; it is not yes or no, but yes and no, not love or hate but love and hate, not alternating or in sequence but at the same time. At this point she is feeling better and worse, more hopeful and more hopeless, all*

105

at once. Hence the continuous inner tumult.)

GAF: Despite your doubts, I wonder if you aren't just a little more hopeful than before?

Janis: Uh . . . yeah I suppose. But you're going on vacation in two weeks. What am I going to do? I can't do this alone. When I leave here today it'll be like every other time. I'll be scared and get to feeling hopeless, and by tonight I won't even exist. *(She starts breathing heavily with increased anxiety).* I can feel it right here now. *(Pointing to her stomach).*

GAF: Let's talk about my vacation and make some arrangements. First, we will have one of my colleagues see you while I'm away. Second, if it becomes necessary, I can be reached on the phone. Third, you should think about setting up a schedule of events for this time—you know, specific dates and times for whatever appropriate activities you choose, like visiting with friends, reading, taking in a play or concert, volunteer work in town. This will bring some needed predictability into your life and reduce your anxiety. Fourth, we can make a mild tranquilizer available for stressful moments, and something else to help you sleep. Okay?

Janis: *(A little relieved but still apprehensive.)* Yeah . . . that feels a little better. *(She still looks worried and is obviously thinking about my vacation and it's affect on her.)*

GAF: And if you need something to keep the feeling of realness and of being connected, you could try keeping a daily journal of your thoughts and feelings.

Janis: Yeah? I like that, I could do that. Yeah. (*Now Janis is having a moment of hope as she thinks maybe things will work out.*) Thanks Doc.

GAF: Okay.

Janis: See you Friday. (*Lingers, then reluctantly leaves.*)

Janis will have trouble while I'm on vacation. Her experience of my absence will result in irrational, intense feelings of abandonment and rage. She will make several suicidal gestures. On my return, she will act out in various ways, including missing the first session.

Session 28.

Janis misses our first scheduled session after I return from vacation. The next day she leaves word with my answering service that she will make the next session. The next session she enters without comment, but her face tells the story.

She is somber and aloof, her clothes are more colorful and psychedelic than ever, and she has gained some weight. After a period of time when it becomes clear that Janis is maintaining an angry silence, I offer a greeting. Therapy with this kind of patient requires constant attention to the tendency to distort reality, act impulsively, and promote further chaos in her life. Thus the patient will be helped by drawing her attention to the nature of the therapeutic process and to our agreement about her responsibility to collaborate with the therapist.

GAF: Good afternoon.

Janis: *(silence)*

GAF: *(After a few more minutes)* You missed your scheduled session on Monday.

Janis: Man. What do you think? Things happened. I've gained ten pounds. I've been using heavy and I get drunk every goddamn night. I needed something to get through. Man, you don't know what it's like. I drank and shot up and balled my brains out. I didn't think I'd see you anymore. It still feels that way, even though I see you there. Like . . . it's just that . . . I felt so hopeless. I was ready to cash it in Sunday night. I ended up in the emergency room—booze and smack. One of the guys in the band found me. The doctor at the hospital said I almost died. It's so confusing and I'm so tired . . . so tired. And I know you have a right to take a vacation, and I knew you were coming back, but it still felt like you were gone for good. *(Janis is agitated and angry and scared.)*

GAF: And that made you angry at me. So you didn't come and didn't call.

Janis: Are you serious? I was in the goddamn emergency room. What do you expect? I know it doesn't make sense . . . you were gone and I said to myself, fuck him. He's like all the rest, never coming through, never there when you need them, always promising but never ready to deliver. But I called Tuesday anyway, so what's the big deal?

GAF: Well, you didn't call on Sunday. *(I persist here in describing the facts about her self-destructive behavior without any intention of determining the reasons for it at this time. The point is to make clear that regardless of why she took the actions she did, we cannot work on them if she doesn't come. The message is that she is has a major responsibility for how well her therapy works. As one of the many types of patients I've encountered, Janis is very impulsive, so the structure and requisite psychotherapy are used to provide some containment of her actions so that the therapy can proceed.)*

Janis: But I almost died. How could I call? Jeez!

GAF: I'm referring to the time before you made the decision to take the drugs and alcohol. You know what happens to you when you take drugs. But you didn't follow the agreement made at the beginning of our work together. You were supposed to call me and let me know that you were going to get high, and therefore you weren't coming on Monday.

Janis: Jeez, you expected me to call and tell you that I was planning to overdose? Are you crazy? Why the fuck would I do that? *(Expressing disbelief, she can't imagine how I arrived at my position.)*

GAF: Well, let's review our agreement about the requirements for your work here. It is necessary for the treatment process that you assume responsibility for your life and actions. This form of treatment *(psychoanalytic psychotherapy)* can only work if we meet regularly and you can't do that if you take actions of any kind that prevent it. So we have to agree on the basic preconditions necessary for this form of therapy. *(I am not expecting Janis to give up her suicidal,*

112

self-destructive behavior—that wouldn't work. I am trying to be clear that for her treatment to be successful she must show up so that her actions can be examined and understood.)

Janis: Okay, okay. Jeez!

GAF: Well, let's see what we do know. You are prone to impulsive actions and some of these include suicidal behaviors that we cannot dismiss as empty or accidental. We must consider you at great risk. Thus, I expect as one of the preconditions for therapy that whenever you are feeling at risk, no matter what the cause, you go directly to a hospital. *(Here Janis is being apprised that I cannot collude with her wish to be treated in a magical way and be saved by an omnipotent therapist.)*

Janis: So. I went to a hospital.

GAF: Yes, but that was after you overdosed. What I'm saying is this: if you're feeling suicidal and feel unable to control it, then you must go to a hospital. If you feel suicidal and yet still in control, then come to our next session and we'll talk about it.

Janis: What if I've already taken stuff?

GAF: The idea is to do something while you're still conscious and able. If you lose control and act suicidal but are still conscious, then you must call 911 or family or police and go to the hospital. There you'll be evaluated as to the need for further hospitalization, just as the ER doctors did on Sunday.

Janis: Well, why can't <u>you</u> evaluate me then?

GAF: Because once you're out of control, someone

else needs to do that. In outpatient therapy my job is to help you toward understanding your problems. If I become involved with managing all of the legal and administrative issues that go along with suicide attempts, I can't fulfill my responsibilities as your outpatient therapist.

Janis: *(After mulling over my comments)* Well, I guess you're the expert. What do we do now? *(Here Janis is feeling helped by the clarity and firmness of my response. She feels more protected from her own actions because my expectations provide her with some structure sorely needed to help contain her own self-destructive impulses.)*

GAF: I had other thoughts about your actions while I was away.

Janis: Yeah? What?

GAF: You could have called but didn't. Dr. Brau was available, but you didn't choose to call her. What can we make of it—of your reluctance to call for help when you felt so bad?

Janis: *(Wrinkles nose and looks away)* I don't know . . . maybe I just didn't think of it.

GAF: Is that the case? Or maybe you were unwilling to call?

Janis: Yeah, that too. I don't feel good about being so needy. I just I hate how pathetic I am. I told you before, I can't even get through a fucking day without calling your office just to listen to your voice on a machine. It's pathetic. Do you know how humiliating that is? At first I was okay, but then ugh. Even that didn't work. I tried things—like working 20 hours a day. I even went to the goddamn movies for chrissakes. But nothing works. I hate calling, I <u>hate</u> it. I feel so stupid, and I don't even get to talk to you, just the fucking machine. (*Janis sinks deeper into the chair as if needing to be enveloped by it. Long silence*). Jeez! I gotta have things, people around. Can't you understand, it's like . . . I have people around all day until I go home. If there's no one home or hanging out, I'm . . . it's, I don't know, unbearable! I really, really feel . . . uh, like nothing, like I'm not there, not alive. I need my friends around all the time. You think my life is too hectic, you think partying when I'm exhausted is strange. (*In a louder and more pleading voice*). Well without them <u>there's nothing</u>! Without you being there, nothing exists! If you're not looking at me or talking to me in person, you don't exist, I don't exist. Can't you understand, can't anybody understand? (*Janis is sobbing uncontrollably. When alone, she cannot have an internal dialogue with the therapist or have a sense of connection or relationship with the therapist because she cannot hold onto any inner "representation" or image of the therapist without the therapist's actual presence. Here is the dilemma and the terror of "object inconstancy", and to some, the true meaning of hell—no internal objects to immunize against the experience of "nothingness."*)

GAF: (*Silence. Let Janis become more consciously aware of the dead zone and its influence on her behavior. The therapist's silent attention offers soothing, nonintrusive company.)*

Janis: (*Janis calms down after a while, but then hopelessness descends.*) I can't do this. I can't do this anymore. I'm so tired, just tired. What do you want. . .what do you expect me to do? I never feel any different. Do you have any idea how it really is? I always feel like this and . . . I'm always thinking about . . . *(Silence)*

GAF: Suicide. You always have thoughts of suicide?

Janis: Yes. You know, huh? *(Silence)*.

GAF: Yes. I know that no matter how well you appear to be, you are never far from feeling the nothingness and the impulse to self-destruct. (*But we have an agreement, right?*)

Janis: (*Relieved to learn that I do know of her vulnerability*).   It's always there. I always feel deserted. Everybody leaves. Linda's in England. Seth left, Chris left, David left. You left. Where the fuck is everybody going? (*It is Janis's "internal objects" that are leaving. She feels as if she is virtually alone in the universe unless the significant people in her life are readily accessible so she can renew her experience of them.*)

GAF: You can't take your experience of them with you, sort of hold on to them in your mind? Feel them there in your mind?

Janis: You mean , like <u>see</u> them? Yeah, man. But they're not, uh . . . like anything, not real. Kinda like ghosts.

GAF: So your experiences with them don't last long after you've been with them? You have no good feeling thinking of them?

Janis: Of course not, how can I? They aren't real. I'm not even sure they're there. They're like . . . like . . . I don't know. It's just, I leave here and I get along for about a day or two, then what am I supposed to do? Camp on your doorstep? *(Brief silence)*. What do you want from me? I can't do this—it's too hard. Do you . . . can you like, have people in your mind? You can do that? *(Janis derives no benefit from any representations of people that may be in her mind. There is no feeling, no emotional connection to those representations. Unlike most of us who do have feelings and some sense of attachment to these internal images, Janis has none. The images are lifeless. They cannot soothe. They leave her in a dead zone. This is a kind of object inconstancy*

121

called "object impermanence," where the representation is present without the feelings that are normally associated with them. The result is the experience of lifelessness that Janis is describing).

GAF: Most people can.

Janis: Jeez. *(Often people in the dead zone do not understand that others do not have the same existential experience as they do.)*

GAF: So are there other reasons why when you were feeling this way you didn't call?

Janis: What do you mean?

GAF: That at a time when you felt so bad, so suicidal, that you chose not to call?

Janis: I couldn't. I told you it was hard . . . humiliating. *(As she sadly realizes her state of affairs, she sinks*

122

even deeper into the softness of the chair.)

GAF: So it's death before revealing your need or vulnerability, even to me?

Janis: Jeez. You are a real pain in the ass. You never let up. You really like this work? People like me—fucked up, wasted, worried, weird people who can't get their shit together . . . day after day you listen to this stuff. Jeez!

GAF: *(Janis will ultimately experience my calm, staying focused approach as soothing and helpful in reducing her confusion and despair).* Mmnn.

Janis: What of it?

GAF: I see the that by not calling me or Dr. Brau when you were in such a state, that you must have been saying forget it, it's too humiliating to call. Better to trip or get zonked. Don't let him

123

know you're in trouble.
He took off. The hell
with him.

Janis: Well . . . you did. I
know, I know, it's
crazy. Jesus. (*Long
silence*). I was felt
despair and I couldn't
make a move. Like I
was in a dream, a
nightmare. I know you
have a right to take a
vacation.

GAF: Despair and
hopelessness. They
discourage anything
you do to manage your
needs by making the
dangers seem
insurmountable, by
confusing the real
picture. By keeping you
from calling.

Janis: Yeah. Why does that
happen?

GAF: Perhaps they offer relief
from the struggle.

Janis: What's so bad about
that? Death would be a
relief.

GAF: Because at the same

time you're courting death you're also seeking life.

Janis: Yeah, that's right. I'm guess I am a real pain in the ass to you, huh? How <u>do</u> you stand it, seeing people like me? Don't you feel like telling me to fuck off? *(Her face slowly breaks into a smile, now teasing and checking at the same time).*

GAF: Are you feeling that way about yourself?

Janis: Yeah, most of the time I feel like shit.

GAF: Maybe you anticipate from me what you feel about yourself?

Janis: *(Long Silence)* No. I never really think of you as being . . . anything. Like you're . . . not . . . like not judging. You, you're not . . . human—no I don't mean that, but it's as though you're not real . . . **and** super real at the same time. I don't know what I'm saying. Man this is hard. *(My reliability and consistency of attitude and response are critical to her sense of being real. As far as she is concerned, in me there will be one object in her life which she can experience as constant, and therefore real. This problem is not typical dependency. Janis functions quite independently. Rather, it is about having no feeling for her internal objects, no sense of them being there and real, so that she can have them when alone. Their absence leaves her alone to deal with the incoherent dread of the dead zone).*

GAF: Both real and not real at the same time?

Janis: Yes, yes! It's all fucked up, doc. I get so confused, all I can think of is booze and smack and . . . and shit. *(Shakes her head)* I had a dream this morning, I

126

mean actually it was more like, I 'm not sure, maybe around one o'clock this afternoon, just before I woke. But it's like uh, I 'm uh, I don't think . . . I want to tell you. It won't be mine anymore. It'll be gone. *(Here Janis reveals the tenuous nature of her connections to objects and to herself. The dream is part of her current self-experience and has become concretized as if it had physical existence. To reveal it is to give a part of her self away.)* I'm so tired, doc, just so tired. *(Long sigh)*

GAF: If you tell me it'll be gone? Why wouldn't it be that we would both have it? *(Such an idea doesn't often occur to her with respect to such deeply personal, inner experiences.)*

Janis: Oh! Gee that's cool, man. Yeah, we could share it, you think? Huh? Ya think? That'd

127

be cool. Okay, okay. I was in some strange place, this was the dream. And it was weird, man—I mean the whole thing was weird. Outa sight. It was San Francisco, like out in Haight-Ashbury you know, my scene, man. There were a lot of people on the street walking around, socializing. I didn't know any of them. I talked to some of them and they didn't even look at me, they didn't even see me, *(In a squeaky, high pitched voice reflecting her tension)* Didn't even see me! That's my scene, my scene. I mean, jeez. How could they not know me? So I'm next to this . . . guy. I stand right in front of him. He looks at me and doesn't smile or anything. All of a sudden he turns into, uh, like a wizard, with a dark blue cape and hat and black eyes that could burn a hole through steel. But I'm curious and not afraid much. So I say something—hello I think. He doesn't say anything, just stares at me. *(Becoming very animated while recounting her dream, Janis' begins to speak much faster, almost frenetically.)*

Now I'm getting afraid, then I get angry and ask him what the fuck he's looking at. I don't know whether to get away or punch him. He still doesn't say anything and I'm confused. I reach over to touch his cape and my hand goes right through him, like he's a shadow, a silhouette or something . . . supernatural. I'm still calm now and I try to touch him again, and he becomes sticky, and I can't get free. My hand's pulled in, then my arm, and then I panic. It feels like I'm going to be . . . to sink into him. But as soon as I yank my hand back, I'm free. And he's still just, just standing there looking at me. And I'm not scared anymore. I woke up scared but then I wasn't. It was really weird, but I felt okay that day, for a while. So . . .what'd ya think? Am I crazy or what? (*Janis is on the edge of her seat.*)

GAF: When did you have this dream?

Janis: The night after I missed my appointment.

GAF: After your office called to cancel your appointment?

Janis: The next night. After you called to confirm today's appointment.

GAF: Uh huh. What comes to mind when you remember the dream?

Janis: I don't know. It was fucking wild. And scary. And way out. The wizard was one scary cat. I felt okay even though I was afraid. That doesn't make any sense does it? The scene—I don't get those people.

GAF: The people who didn't
see you?

Janis: Yeah, man. How could
they not see me? I know
everybody in Haight-
Ashbury, man.

GAF: How did you feel in the
dream, when they didn't
see you?

Janis: Hey, jeez! I don't know,
it . . . that was a real
bummer, man. They
didn't even see me. I
got distracted by the
wizard, but they were
like . . . almost like, uh .
. . ghosts or something.
But I thought to myself,
in the dream, don't they
know me, or are they
snubbing me? Well,
fuck them. And I was
going to find somebody
or something, I dunno,
when I ran into the
wizard.

GAF: Have you felt that way
before, that you aren't
being seen?

Janis: Yeah.   (*slowly*)

Sometimes I get pretty down when there's no one around or talking to me and I think, nobody gives a fuck, why is everybody down on me? I can't stand being ignored.

GAF: Uh huh. What comes to mind about the wizard?

Janis: That fuckin' wizard—ya know, his eyes were like pure black. Evil, but soft, too. I'm thinking evil, but then I also think . . . he was cool, man, like with the dark blue duds, and there was something softer in his eyes even though they were shiny black. The blue cape was like superman's in the comics, ya know? And when I went through his arm with my hand, I think I was more surprised than scared. No, I was scared too. At first I thought, he's gonna kill me. Then I thought, maybe he's friendly. Then that sticky shit, that was weird, I mean it was

way out man. I was
panicked. But it's
funny, it didn't hurt or
anything. But I was
scared. Terrified.
*(Clearly excited by this
dreamwork, Janis
awaits my comments
with great anticipation.)*

GAF: Black, evil eyes?

Janis: Yeah, black and shiny.
Sort of like yours. I
thought that his eyes
were evil, then I
thought, soft, then I got
confused. Now that I
think of it, I felt a lot
like I do in here
sometimes. Oh, jeez, I
just realized, for a
moment in the dream I
had this uh, I dunno . . .
this idea flashed . . .
that his eyes could see
into my mind and that
he knew everything
about me. *(Brief
silence)*. I think I wasn't
sure whether to be
scared or not.

GAF: And the dark blue?

Janis: I don't know. It was not
too dark, more of a

medium blue, just like the color of these chairs. Oh shit. The wizard—that's you right? Jesus! I can't believe this stuff. Oh, I just had another flash. The wizard in his blue cape makes me think of you in the blue chair somehow. Jeez. I felt just as mixed up about him as I do about you. Am I right? Is that possible?

GAF: Mmmm. So everybody ignores you, but he bores in on you with his eyes?

Janis: Yeah, isn't that weird? Nobody ignores me. I'm hard to ignore. My mother always said I needed a lot of attention when I was a kid. So I don't get why I should dream about not getting any. And that wizard. He was giving me plenty of attention and I guess now, looking at it, that I wasn't sure about him—not sure about. I don't know about what. I think there was a time in the dream I felt he was okay. But when my hand went through his arm, that was scary. I got all confused. (*Brief silence*). And the stickiness—it was like I wouldn't be able to get loose, like I'd be pulled in and swallowed up. Jeez! The wizard, the wizard, he's you, man, he's you, isn't he? (*Stares off blankly*) I know it is. His eyes, he could see right through me. You . . . see right through me. Sometimes I am afraid of you just like I was of him. But I . . . you're not, you haven't done anything to make me afraid. Except I need you too much. I could just disappear, like whoosh, just like my hand going through his, your arm. (*Janis has once again described the need-fear dilemma. Her psychological mindedness and ability to perceive the hidden meaning in the dream, for example, point to a more favorable prognosis.)* You're the only one who knows what's happening with me. Without you, I'm nothing, not real, like in the dream when nobody paid attention to me. They weren't ignoring me. I wasn't real, I wasn't really there to them. Only the wizard was there and I'd be alone without him. And I was sure he was there, but I was angry at him for scaring me. Then when I tried to touch him and went right through him, Jesus. Even he wasn't really there. And so I wasn't really there . . . or anywhere. Or maybe I was him when I touched him. I don't know . . . *(Silence)*

GAF: You're scared and angry at how much you depend on me. When I left on vacation, you became frightened at how alone you felt, how alienated from yourself and everyone else you felt as in the dream when no one noticed you. You became enraged with me for abandoning you, and so you saw me as dark and evil and you decided to lash out at the wizard. But your lash turned into a touch because you also needed me and didn't want to destroy me. Then you feared that maybe I wasn't real, shown by your going right through me. So you expressed your rage by getting high and not coming to the first appointment on my return. (*Here I attempt to weave the dream interpretation with her reality to help put it together.*)

Janis: I'm really fucked up, huh? (*She seems sad and subdued, but not for very long*). So how come I'm fucked up like this? Why me, huh? Why? (*more silence*) Ya know, doc, I get so tired, so tired. *(Janis looks depleted as she often does in sessions. Although she rebounds at other times, I have a*

sense that her struggle with the deadness is pulling her down. I am concerned that she may not have the endurance for the years of psychotherapy needed.)
I *do* think that Jimi had it right . . . it's just too hard, too fucking hard. (*Another brief silence*). Let me ask you what you think. If you were me, and you knew what you know now, would you feel, like, uh, cool, like . . . hopeful? Come on, doc, would you? Would you? (*Desperately hoping for words that would change the way she feels.*)

GAF: Yes.

Janis: You'd say that anyway. Why yes? Why? I can't make it through the day without booze, smack, sex, or some other shit. My mind's all messed up and I look like shit. I'm fat and I can't hold onto anybody. They all left. Everyday is exhausting. I already feel dead. So why should I feel hopeful? Why? Dead seems like a pretty good idea—no more of this. So tell me why I should hope. *(Janis is truly feeling hopeful and hopeless at one and the same time. She is prodding me in an attempt to resolve her ambivalence).*

GAF: Here is a good example of how you trap yourself in a no-way-out scenario. If I tell you there's hope, your hopelessness will not let you believe that I believe it. That's what hopelessness does: make us all disbelieve. If, on the other hand, I agree that it is hopeless, then your hopefulness will cause you to disbelieve. You try to keep away from either place—neither hope, nor hopeless. The danger of hope or hopelessness is the same—they can both lead you closer to the same dreadful, avoid-at all-costs experience. Hopelessness can lead to death. But so can hope because something of you seems to die everyday when you experience the overwhelming intensity of your human needs followed by the threat of abandonment and the terrifying nothingness when those needs aren't met. So you try to stay in between, that is, to stay in neither place, to stay nowhere.

Janis: (*Janis slumps more completely in the chair and looks at me. This bit of interpretation has caught her interest in that it seems to be an accurate description of something she feels but has never quite understood.*) Yeah, I do, I do. It's better than . . . (*she shakes her head and slowly begins to cry softly, unable to find words.*)

GAF: Better than . . .

Janis: I don't know. I read

Sarte a long time ago. It left me feeling weird, like he knew something about me—the despair, the despair of life. He . . . it was about despair and I remember thinking then that it was about, too. And you . . . you know even more about what's in my head. *(Long silence)*. Better? It's better than the . . . nothing . . . better than the confusion better than the mess in my head. It's just that I can't stay there, keep away from despair for long. And I hate the longing, the need for love. It's too painful. Just as you said, everybody leaves and then it's . . . .*(There is a perceptible shudder as Janis tries to describe the indescribable, the sense of annihilation which grips her in the face of object-connection failures. She cannot hold on to the connection to anyone. Her life forces are slowly being destroyed.*

141

*Her will to be, to fight
the forces of death and
to grip life is being
depleted. She is slipping
into the abyss. I am
touched by her inability
to feel life and at the
same time her feeling
life so intensely that it
overwhelms her with
anxiety. She is not able
to move between the
extremes of emptiness
and intensity and draw
on both creatively,
except perhaps when
she is at her work. I
fear for her survival.*)

GAF: Like death?

Janis: Worse. Where the fuck
is everybody going?
Why do they all leave?
You can't count on
anybody.

GAF: Perhaps you help
people to leave.

Janis: What do you mean?

GAF: You've told me that
some of your
boyfriends left because
they didn't like the way
you fooled around with

other guys, and that others didn't like your moods, the drinking, and the drugs. If your goal was to have a close, intimate relationship, why didn't you adjust your behavior to get it?

Janis: Well shit, doc, I can't relate to that. I have to be true to my game, not theirs. I like having fun and doing what feels good. *(Janis now shifts emotions and actively begins to defend her behavior. As is often the case with borderlines of this sort, it's difficult for her to accept blame for her problems.)*

GAF: So you need or value the drugs, alcohol, and multiple partners more than a close, one-to-one relationship?

Janis: Jesus, why do you put it that way? I just have to do my own thing, man, that's all. Why are you blaming me? I can't help it if the cats are never there when you

143

need them. You just can't trust them. They always let you down. *(Becoming more annoyed, and then sulking.)*

GAF: So it's just the way it is? Your actions have little to do with all the disappointment you have about relationships? You're just a very unlucky chick?

Janis: Well, maybe I am a ballbuster sometimes. I just want people to be sincere and to have a good time. *(Smiles proudly).* Some cats can't handle it.

GAF: Or maybe you feel threatened, as we've discussed before—fear of the intensity of your longing and the terror of being abandoned can cause you to short circuit a relationship you may really want before you can feel the dread of being separated. Even a short separation from the person can cause you great anxiety once you become attached to them.

Janis: You think I sabotage relationships?

GAF: Don't you think so?

Janis: I don't know. I've never thought of it that way. I can relate to being needful. Sometimes when I need something, when I need to get down, man, I can get goin', get groovin' and nothing can stop me. Ya know? Like I can't stand being . . . like stopped.

GAF: When you're needy, you're impulsive and persistent?

Janis: Right. (*For borderline personalities, impulsivity is often a defense against anxiety*).

GAF: Does that happen with people. That is, do you feel the need to act impulsively, for

example,   sexually,
when   you're   with
someone you're getting
close to?

Janis: (*Slowly*). You mean like
when I ball some guy I
just met while I'm in a
relationship   with
someone else?

GAF: Yes.   Doesn't   that
usually help to sabotage
the relationship?

Janis: Yeah,   (*somewhat
glumly*) I guess so. I
don't know. I mean,
jeez, what . . . why is
everything so hard? I
just need a lot of action
man, that's all.

GAF: What are you feeling
when you go looking
for   sexual   liaisons
while in the midst of a
love affair?

Janis: I don't know. Just feel
the need to pick up
some new talent and get
it on. (*Clearly annoyed
and a bit confused, she
wrinkles her brow.*)

GAF: Is it hard for you to

146

understand why that behavior may damage an existing relationship?

Janis: I . . . no I guess not. It's just that I have such an appetite.

GAF: Could it be that you become apprehensive or agitated in some way and impulsively seek relief by distracting yourself with new stimulation?

Janis: Yeah, I get bored man. It's fucking boring sometimes.

GAF: What times?

Janis: I don't know, different times for chrissakes.

GAF: How about when someone you are close to leaves you for a while? Or just leaves the room when you're having a disagreement?

Janis: (*Ponders my question*) Well, yeah. Like when Seth took off last month after I got pissed at him.

He just left and I went nuts. I stayed smashed for three days and balled my brains out. That what you mean?

GAF: What happened to you when he left? I mean, what was it like for you when he left before you got to drinking and so forth?

Janis: You mean right after?

GAF: Yes.

Janis I . . . I'm not sure. It just seemed as though I was completely alone, ya know what I mean—as though there wasn't anybody else.

GAF: How was that for you to feel?

Janis: It was horrible. I felt horrible and . . . and panicked. *(For Janis, like others in the dead zone, when people are gone, they are gone— do not exist anymore, are not real.)* I couldn't stand it, just couldn't stand it, him just

148

leaving like that.

GAF: Didn't you expect him to be angry at your behavior?

Janis: I don't know, I didn't think about it.

GAF: How come? *(I am working here to let Janis see the contradiction between her complaints that no one sticks around so that she is always lonely on the one hand, and her behaviors that are so destructive to intimate personal relationships on the other.)*

Janis: How come? I don't know, jeez. I guess.

GAF: Maybe we can discuss this further next time.

Janis: Fuck.

In these and hundreds of sessions to follow, Janis tries with great persistence to grasp the deadness and contain its effects on her personality. No one can predict the outcome, but if after a number of years (five to eight or more) she is to be able to organize a structured lifestyle and she uses the therapist as well

149

as she has in these sessions, then her world might gain some measure of stability and peace. It is likely that her talents will remain intact and that a reasonably gratifying, "safe" relationship will develop. She will remain unpredictable and impulsive over the years, but nevertheless slowly improve her ability to control the torment of the dead zone.

Chapter Five: Jim Morrison—Poet, Shaman, Lizard King

"I am the lizard king, I can do anything"

Like Janis, Jim was eventually destroyed by his inability to escape the dead zone; and like Janis he was far more than his searching, disharmonious and morose frame of mind might suggest. Jim possessed a deeply intellectual and complex mind, capable of synthesizing wildly discordant experiences and ideas. He created a musical style that captured the universal longing for meaning that he hoped was hidden in the mystical, in the arcane. Unable to find relief from the alienation that was his constant companion, he sought escape through the chaos he experienced as maximum entropy. From that peculiar vantage point, the very existence of order and its accompanying rules blocked the opportunity to "break on through" the chaos he endured, and find the meaning that might have ended his despair.

The life of Jim Morrison has been amply chronicled in several books that have been most helpful to our study: *Break On Through* by James Riordan and Jerry Prochnicky; *No One Here Gets Out Alive* by Jerry Hopkins and Danny Sugerman; and *Riders On The Storm* by John Densmore, The Doors' drummer. As we reviewed all the material on Jim Morrison, we tried to look beyond the intellectual brilliance he frequently flashed through his rather odd and obnoxious behavior. All of his biographers presented a portrait of him as a taunting, teasing, hostile, oppositional man whose embrace of the dark side reflected his own deeply embedded despair and alienation. However much he repelled us, we could not help but be touched by the depth of his suffering, a suffering he tried to relieve with his heavy drinking, constant drug abuse and often sadistic behavior. Few passages from any biography were as painful to read and as revealing as this one from *Break On Through*:

> A diary of Jim's, thought to be
> from around this period (at the

> end of his life, in Paris), is
> riddled with a sense of
> helplessness—scrawled
> passages of desperation in lines
> like 'God help me, God help
> me, God help me' scribbled
> over and over again, filling
> entire pages. It is as though he
> cast away the last vestiges of
> caution, finally delving into the
> one substance that he had held
> back from before (Riodan and
> Prognicky 1991, 461).

But, of course, no one was really capable of helping him at that time.

Jim

Jim was raised in the south, in Florida, New Mexico and Washington, D.C.), by a conventional middle class family. His parents held to the societal values characteristic of the 1950's, were supportive of their progeny and encouraged their higher education. His biographers did not note any abuse, alcoholism, or significant family disturbances. Like Janis', Jim's family consistently and patiently tried to understand and help, though Jim repeatedly rejected the basic values of his family.

Well read and possessing superior intelligence, both had read poets such as Corso, Ferlinghetti, McClure, and Jack Kerouac (Amburn 1992, 141). However, Jim was drawn to the more arcane, darker-toned literature of Plutarch, Baudelaire, Kafka, Rimbaud, Joyce, Balzac, Cocteau, and Moliere. Jim was witty, quick, rebellious, oppositional and tended toward the outrageous.

Neither appeared to have clear goals in mind as they graduated from high school. Although both had finished school with good grades, they consistently under- achieved, using only part of their intelligence, or using their intelligence inconsistently and unevenly. Possessing undefined or unrealistic plans about their futures, both appeared to have attained their rock star status by a confluence of unusual circumstances: the emerging, youthful, student counterculture of the 60's whose *behaviors* often "looked" just like those acted out by Janis and Jim; their own rapidly expanding interest in radically new life experiences; and the considerable artistic talent each possessed for developing music.

In L.A., Janis was known as "the female Jim Morrison," and in San Francisco, *The Doors* were known as "Hollywood's version of Big Brother," the group Janis first sang with (Amburn 1992, 133). Both artists used and continued to use drugs and alcohol until they died, were *lost souls* without solid identities, could not sustain stable, nonexploitative relationships, died at 27, and lived the whole of their lives in the dead zone.

Though similar in numerous ways, their lives could otherwise be characterized as different in one very significant aspect: their individual attempts to escape the dead zone. Janis tried to escape the dead zone by openly embracing hope, searching for affection, sensuality, eroticism, intense emotion. Her focus was on love and sex. That she was unable to assimilate all that she encountered had tragic, deadly consequences.

Jim, on the other hand, looked for an exit from the dead zone by joining forces with darkness and destruction, by embracing the "other side" and seeking to "break on through" to another level of experience by out-deviling the devil. Thus, he focused on sex and violence. Put differently, the same underlying forces that generated Janis' obsession with people, sex and life, were the same forces that moved Jim to embrace demons, discord, and death.

Background

James Douglas (after Douglas MacArthur, the World War II general and hero) Morrison was born in 1943 to parents who were "kind, affable and upwardly mobile," (Riordan and Prochnicky 1991, 26). Jim's father was one of three children, born in Florida to a conservative laundry owner, something of a goody-goody in high school and rather popular with the girls. He later saw action in World War II as a carrier pilot, and in Korea where he coordinated carrier based air attacks, subsequently commanding an aircraft carrier and eventually being promoted to rear admiral, (Hopkins and Sugerman 1980, 9).

Hopkins and Sugerman describe Morrison's mother as "one of five children of the slightly kooky, fun-loving daughter of a maverick lawyer from Wisconsin." (Hopkins and Sugerman, 13). She met Jim's father at a navy dance around the time the Japanese were preparing to bomb Pearl Harbor. Riordan and Prochnicky claim that neighbors remember her as an "attractive, witty and active person who had a few oddities of her own." She is described as something of a nature lover and beachcomber, often using a metal detector. She would collect sand dollars and sea shells used to craft home decorations.

Neither parent spanked the children (Jim had a younger brother and sister). Verbal admonitions were used instead, with his mom being the disciplinarian. Away much of the time, Jim's father fluctuated between treating his children as recruits and exercising little parental authority, choosing instead to let his wife apply whatever discipline might be necessary.

As a result of Jim's father's duty assignments, his family was forced to move from station to station: Jim lived in Pensacola, Melbourne, and Clearwater, Florida, twice in both Washington, D.C. and Albuquerque, New Mexico, and once each in Los Altos, Claremont, and Alameda, California before attending high school in Alexandria, Virginia. These moves came with little warning, leading to a nomadic existence and providing no feeling of consistency in Jim's life.

On the strength of that feature of Jim's background, some have suggested that this travelogue lifestyle and the absent father left too little structure in Jim's life and contributed to his problems as an adult. The frequent moves that are so much a part of military life can often create stress for a family, and perhaps did for Jim, though his brother and sister appear to have emerged from that experience unaffected.

To claim that Jim Morrison was a difficult child is to understate significantly what his biographers have written. Riordan and Prochnicky write that Jim "grew to be a minor terror within his family," (Riordan and Prochnicky, 56) a hell-raiser, demanding attention, causing much embarrassment, and resenting his siblings. Hopkins and Sugerman describe in every painful detail how Jim would physically and psychologically torment his brother, Andy, (Hopkins and Sugerman, 30). Neither his sister nor his high school girlfriend escaped his sadism. In a pattern that continued throughout his short life, he mistreated and often abused his mother, women he picked up, several girlfriends (including Janis Joplin) and his most enduring paramour, Pamela Courson.

Jim's intelligence apparently made it easy for him to be difficult and rebellious in school. He would not work consistently on assignments and was perceived to be a "brilliant recluse," preferring to study unusual, abstruse subjects, dark, mystical ideas, and historical figures. He spent some time researching information about reptiles, his intelligence enabling him to produce excellent reports while at the same time rejecting conventional material and authority of any kind. His biographers write of his early oppositional behavior, referring to such outrageous behaviors as yelling out "hey motherfucker" to passersby in the hall during the middle of a class, or giving outlandish excuses for tardiness (e.g., he had been robbed on the way or he had had an operation for a brain tumor). He delighted in challenging teachers with complex ideas and often used his wits to try to humiliate them. For example, he would delve deeply into unassigned but sophisticated readings and proceed to quiz his teachers. He constantly attempted one-up-man-ship, believing himself to be smarter than they. Immersing himself in philosophy and existential literature, he was very familiar with Hume, Montaigne, Sartre, Nietzsche, Kafka, Greek and Roman history, and he especially admired Alexander the Great. He was also fascinated by the pornographic and violent dime store novels he read constantly.

Jim is further described as an attention-seeking, sullen, rowdy, uncooperative, exceptionally intelligent loner who rejected the idea of being anything, and violently resisted conforming to conventional standards. In college, he conducted himself as he did in high school. Early on, his roommates asked him to leave because of his unrelenting self-centered, inconsiderate and exploitative behaviors (refusing to lower his loud music, taking others' clothes without permission, not carrying his share of the workload, and so on).

John Densmore writes about similar complaints and about how irresponsible Jim was before and during performances. *The Doors* , Ray Manzarek, John Densmore and Robby Krieger, were living on the edge in their association with Jim as much as they were in the music they played together. They felt as a group that they were unusual because the music they played was "on the edge" of acceptable music: spontaneous, raw, and innovative. They creating the music and the mood as they played, experiencing the intensity and breaking down old musical conventions. Morrison called the Doors "sexual politicians." They all accepted that term but invested it with a different meaning than Jim did. They didn't feel what Morrison felt. They used similar language but it referred to different inner experiences.

In college, Jim continued to pursue a wide variety of interests and often found himself drawn to the surrealistic. In keeping to his character, his tastes and interests shifted frequently, depending on what persona he was creating at the time. Jim was charismatic and could draw people into his game, and manipulate them, all the while remaining quite detached from the hostile feelings he generated in others. His early years were prologue to the search that consumed his energies afterward and eventually destroyed him—the search for meaning, for a way to break through the despair of life in the dead zone.

Break On Through: Embracing The Dead Zone

157

Like Janis, Jim used alcohol, drugs and sex in every way he could. He was persistent, and, unlike Janis, sadistic. In these pursuits, some have said that Jim was really testing the bounds of reality, and reminding us where the name "Doors" came from. Morrison was taken with a line from William Blake: "If the doors of perception were cleansed every thing would appear as it is, infinite." Jim's biographers report that he used to say, "there are things known and unknown and in between are the doors".

Aldous Huxley had taken the Blake line and written *The Doors of Perception,* telling of his own attempts to find new levels of mind and consciousness through the use of mescaline. The idea of skirting the edge, of breaking down convention and gaining a cleansed perspective, appears to have captured that part of Jim which sought to "know" the mystical and the visionary. In seeking the mystical and the visionary, he hoped they might offer him a way to "understand the relationship of words to things, of systematic reasoning to the unfathomable mystery which it tries, forever vainly, to comprehend," (Huxley as cited in Hopkins and Sugerman, 45).

Given these propensities, it is not surprising that Jim was drawn to the darker poets and writers such as Edgar Allen Poe, Franz Kafka and especially Arthur Rimbaud. From surrealism, Morrison quickly adopted the notion of reaching into the subconscious and disorder to find order, into illusion to find reality. Rimbaud moved these surrealistic ideas to even greater extremes by seeking the logical from the illogical, and sanity through insanity. Jim pursued sanity through insanity, and in so doing embraced the arcane, the mysterious, the hidden, the inscrutable, the extreme, the illogical, the disordered, and the sensual, (Riordan and Prochnichy, 134). How else could any true understanding take place?

So Jim constantly lived on the edge, being captured by the lure of that mode of living. Sharing with him in that state of *mind, The Doors* performed and lived on the narrow border between the rational and the irrational, the real and the surreal, the known and the unknown.

Jim's efforts to break through the limits of the senses and ordinary experience were not driven by intellectual forces or curiosity, but by the irresistible dread emanating from the dead zone. All who have written about him have made it clear that Jim drank heavily, not for enjoyment but to get drunk. Like Janis, he tried many drugs but eventually settled on heroin. That's not surprising, since both alcohol and heroin obliterate awareness of the dead zone. In spite of the many attempts to escape that terrible destination, the lives of these two artists were overwhelmed by the same dread, the fear and profound terror of the dead zone.

The purpose of Jim's self-destructive substance abuse was not to discover the other side but to *escape* to the other side. He sought to escape the deeply distressing anxiety emanating from an inner world, more lonely for him than if he had grown up somehow without human contact. By behaving in an outrageous and provocative manner, Jim attempted to fill the void, to prevent panic from overwhelming him. Hanging off of the ledge of a tall building, rambling on in a trance like a shaman, cursing his audience, instigating a police officer to arrest him, tormenting a bus driver or a teacher were all actions driven by the same demons. And they were the same demons that plagued Janis. The greater the tension he could generate in the system because of his actions, the less he felt the alienation, despair and dread.

Riordan and Prochnicky discuss Jim's antics this way:

> . . . he never did them
> for publicity. He did them for
> excitement. He got in barroom
> brawls. He swung nude from the
> bell tower at Yale. He played
> matador with the cars on the
> freeway. He challenged cops
> repeatedly and was maced,
> clubbed, and beaten more than
> once (Riordan and Prognicky,

Hopkins and Sugerman write that he was "by his own admission attracted to extremes." They quote Jim as saying, "I think the highest and lowest points are the important ones. All the points in between are, well, in between. I want freedom to try everything—I guess to experience everything at least once."

The real motive, however, for this tragic pattern of excitement-seeking was by no means clear to him. That is, Jim (and Janis) may have been aware of the desire to provoke or create some havoc around them, to experience everything, but they were unaware of the deeper forces and motives which propelled them, and thus had to rationalize their behaviors in some way. Janis said she was just an unconventional type who saw through the hypocrisy of many social values and was doing her own thing. Jim intellectualized and justified his actions by espousing a search for knowledge beyond the realm of the common, into the subconscious, seeking to learn from chaos. Whatever explanation *Jim* may have attached to his behavior, there is overwhelming evidence that his exploration of the other side was a very complex effort of an intelligent but troubled mind to solve his problem: that of living a life without internal objects in the desolation of the dead zone. Life without internal objects is "living a life without the necessary experience-of-oneself-as-real," which can only come from the capacity to *experience* the presence of early significant others within ourselves.

Jim Morrison was once quoted as saying that he felt his imagination was liberated onstage, and Ray Manzarek observes:

> For Jim, being onstage was just about everything. On stage he came alive and was the most exciting and dynamic performer I'd ever seen. He would go through trips onstage . . . you wouldn't believe the

personalities that would come out of him, the intensity that he would speak to the audience (Riordan and Prochnicky, 187).

But perhaps Riordan and Prochnicky themselves offer the best characterization of his performances:

> Watching him sing was like witnessing a man dangling in his own anguish. Seeing him scream, writhe, and whisper his way into a head-on clash with some ultimate truth in song could be truly frightening. Even the most unfeeling in the audience sensed that the sudden shrieks and violent screams came from somewhere deep within the subconscious. (Riordan and Prochnicky, 186)

Morrison acted out on many levels. Not all were entertaining; none were understood. Morrison could ponder the mystical, experiment with concepts, dabble with the notion of creative chaos, and write surreal poetry. But he was a Jekyll and Hyde character— unpredictable, self-destructive, and confused. His alienation from others and from himself was complete, and he experienced it practically from the beginning.

Searching For Jim: Lost Between The Doors

The Shaman

Jim Morrison quit the Doors, we believe, to find himself, to become a person with a solid, continuous self-feeling, to continue the struggle with his increasing alienation from life itself. He needed to find a self. How could he have known that the common developmental task we all face would be forever impossible for him? He knew something was wrong. Before he left to live the remaining months of his life in Paris, he said, "I don't know who I am, I don't know what I'm doing, I don't know what I wanna do . . . I'm gone . . . don't count on me, goodbye." Neither the instigative, thrill-seeking, chaotic, outrageous behaviors, nor the fine intellect and talent could rescue him from the dead zone. His vulnerability to the splitting of experience and to object inconstancy frustrated all his efforts to feel real and stable, to feel okay, and to feel himself to be the same person continuously from moment to moment.

Jim had always sought to find self-definition. This search was marked first by constant attention-seeking as a child. When he still couldn't *feel* his own existence, he then looked to others for the reactions and responses he needed to bolster himself and to provide a reflected sense of self. His troublesome childhood behaviors foreshadowed adolescent and adult misadventures and stimulus seeking. As an adult, he pressed his intellect into serving his search for self. His futile attempts to fashion a "me" for himself included displays of intellectual arrogance, preoccupation with bizarre and esoteric subject matter, and an oppositional, I'm-different-from-everyone-else attitude.

Eventually, Jim tried to fit himself into a life role, hoping to find the self he had always been looking for. Of course, this role had to be intense and special. Only by passing through the doors of perception into the mystical and the unconventional—outside of the world in which he found no solace—might he find himself. Hence his shamanism. And his poetry. And the lizard king.

Much has been made of the incident he witnessed as a child where a truckload of Indians had been injured and killed in an accident. As the medicine man lay dying on the side of the road, his spirit, it is alleged, had entered Jim's body. Though our analysis suggests that we shouldn't attribute very much of anything to that accident, Jim did eventually come to see himself as a shaman, as having the special power to see through the falsehoods of this world into the next, to that world beyond the "doors of perception." Now, according to this rather unconventional account of how Jim came to be the bizarre character he was, people become shamans by experiencing a close call with death or some other deadly trauma followed by rebirth and then instruction regarding the spirit world. Shamans thereafter deal in dreams, visions, reveries, trances, mythology, and spirits. As unique spirits, they can be moody, irritable, depressed, and anxious, as well as emotionally hyper reactive and then isolative.

This occult-like identity fit Jim's needs for a time, and he reveled in it, trying on the identity of a "rock shaman." One article called him "a slithering sorcerer" in response to his shamanist leanings and his famous "I am the lizard king" pronouncements. Music helped this shaman relieve the sickness of the other, enhancing the process of taking on the other's evil by singing in trances and becoming evil's repository. Doors audiences were moved by the arcane and intensely emotional quality of these shamanist rituals, especially when combined with rock music and Morrison's stage presence. How Jim understood himself as he conducted these concerted exercises in emotional tension while instigating chaos was perhaps best summed up in a quote about such a role:

> I am possessed by the spirit of a shaman. I see the role of the artist as shaman and scapegoat. People project their fantasies on to him and their fantasies come alive. By attacking and punishing me people can feel relieved of their impulses. (Riordan and Prochnicky, 192)

In our view, it wasn't the fans who needed to be relieved of their impulses. Failing to recognize the need in himself, Jim projected that need onto the audience. The audiences' reactions were meant to shore up *his* failing self and prevent *his* disintegration of self-feeling. How could he have known that he was squandering his psychological resources on the search for *his* substance, for a feeling of existence, for that nebulous entity called a self? That search turns out to be mostly hopeless for those who live in the dead zone. Whether one refers to it as the "I", the "me", "identity", the "core self", or "self organization", Jim had no grasp of it and at some level knew that. He couldn't find his way based on any internal compass because the one normally used—that abstraction we routinely label "me"—did not exist for him. He was a man without a center, without the inner feeling of a core. His core self (which is created out of the experience of one's own existence) had never been formed. It was lost or unfinished, and thus floating somewhere between the doors of perception in the dead zone.

The Poet

Poets attempt to move people also. They communicate at both conscious and unconscious levels with the audience, presenting their own versions of the meaning of life and death by using language in an uncommon fashion. Jim had often declared himself a poet and he wrote throughout his short life. Several volumes of his work have been published since his death. However his poetry failed to define him. His final notes of despair cited earlier make it quite clear that an integrated sense of self forever eluded him.

That this man of superior intelligence and talent did not find himself in poetry was just another of the tragedies that befell him. From both a literary and a clinical point of view, there is no meaning to be found in Jim's poetry nor in his attempt at film making in college. His poetry and film seem to be a conglomerate of images of sex and death, images which are primitive, erotic, religious, chaotic, exotic, and without recognizable meaning. They seem to have been created out of the distorted fantasies and fragmentary, shifting elements of a mind living in its own hell. The poetry, like the shamanism, was created for dual purposes: to stimulate a feeling of life while living in the dead zone, and to organize an atomized and disordered collection of experiences into something resembling an identity.

Jim Morrison's poems can be widely interpreted not because they are a synthesis of complex ideas and experiences, but rather because they are essentially without meaning except for the tormented confusion they reveal about the mind of the poet himself. His intelligence could not truly help him in this effort, though it did enable him to create a poet's facade as an identity, a "false self" which could only disintegrate from the moment it was constructed. That this was inevitable should not surprise us, since identities do not evolve out of whole cloth. They emerge slowly through internalization of the elements of those personalities, those significant people, in one's early environment. These elements are then "metabolized" in the formation of the real self.

From the very beginning, Jim's vulnerability to *splitting* and *object inconstancy* limited his capacity to internalize the essence of significant others. Thus he could not *feel* himself to be somebody (in the sense that he could literally absorb all of the disparate experiences he so aggressively sought into a formed self) no matter how many poems he wrote, or trances he fell into, or images he provoked in his audiences.

The Lizard King

Jim began his fascination with reptiles in childhood, learning extensively about them. As an adult he came to be known as the lizard king, saying to an audience, " I am the lizard king, I can do anything." Since reptiles commonly evoke fear and a sense of the mysterious, it is clear that Jim was again drawn to the unusual and the occult in summoning the power of reptiles to induce strong reactions. The darker motivations of man are often ascribed to the "reptilian period" of man's evolution. This inscrutable quality of the reptile was a natural attraction for Jim.

He projected his own hopes and fantasies into a reptilian identity, an identity he could feel by wearing the lizard skin suit he had made for himself. No one who saw him wearing that suit in concert will ever forget it.

In his reptilian rapture we might imagine him to be inspired by the imagery of being powerful, scary, and specific—some kind of reality for himself—dark, dangerous and defined. His suit reinforced his sense of being, someone whose presence he hoped to feel. "I am the lizard king " he said over and over again.

Regrettably, the unfinished half of that pronouncement which Jim Morrison could not understand was *"Therefore I am."* Sadly, poignantly, unlike most adolescents who develop normally, he never could answer the question, "Who am I?". But then, few in the dead zone can.

These three pseudo-identities failed to catalyze the identity formation process. Jim desperately needed the emotional stability and soothing that should normally have occurred with the "metabolizing" of the raw materials of personality taken from those childhood caregivers who loved him and taught him. He was without any means of comprehending, or preventing his demise. *Splitting* and *object inconstancy,* however they happen, are not readily understandable or easily treated, regardless of how they occur.

Love Me Two Times: I Can't See Your Face In My Mind

Hopkins and Sugerman write of a phone call from Jim's mother. The Morrisons had not heard from their son for a very long time and were trying to locate him. A friend of Jim's brother, Andy, had been listening to a *Doors* album and recognized Jim's picture on the cover. His mother had called Elektra Records and convinced them that she was indeed his mother, thereby obtaining his phone number. Hopkins and

Sugerman record the following conversation:

Mrs. Morrison: Hello? This is Mrs. Morrison, is Jim there?
Jim: Jim who?
Mrs. Morrison: Jim. Jim Morrison. I'm his mother.
Jim: Yeah? *(The man sounded bored.)*
(Another voice came on the line.) Hello?
Mrs. Morrison: Jim? Oh Jim . . . .
Jim: Yes, Mother . . . .

He replied with a series of grunts and moans to his mother's concerns about his not calling, writing, or even letting them know where he was and that he was all right. She asked him to come home for Thanksgiving dinner with the family. She asked him to get a haircut for his father's sake (now admiral Morrison). He sighed and promised nothing. The others in the room were just listening. Hopkins and Sugerman record that Jim hung up and then said, "I don't want to talk to her ever again."

Jim had once told a reporter upon questioning that his parents were dead. They obviously weren't, and so some of those in the room must have been startled by this phone call from his mother. To Jim—who had great difficulty with *object constancy*, his parents were not *internalized*—they were in his memory but without any sense of realness, nor feeling of attachment. Therefore it was as though they did not exist for him. And because he couldn't *feel* their existence (in the sense described earlier), he couldn't feel his own.

Ironically, the title of one of his songs, "I can't see your face in my mind," reflects his vulnerability to object inconstancy. He simply could not bring to his mind any "emotionally valuable representation" of these early significant people in his life. Essentially, people were experienced by Jim as "objects," lifeless and unreal. Without such a capacity for object relations, he might as well have been living alone on Mars. He could not stay connected to anyone except briefly under conditions of extreme tension or stimulation. We see this in his interaction with all women, including Pamela Courson and

167

Patricia Kennealy.

During his career with the Doors and up until his death, Jim Morrison maintained a "relationship" with Pamela Courson. He had many other liaisons, but always returned to her, and she seems to have treated him in kind. It would take a certain kind of partner to tolerate Jim's destructive behaviors. In startling detail, Riordan and Prochnicky describe (as told by Paul Rothchild, *The Doors*' producer) the typical nature of his relationships with women in his encounter with Janis Joplin:

> She saw this hunk of meat (Jim) and said, 'I want that.' Jim would get drunk most days and this was no exception and as usual he got rude, obnoxious, and violent. He turned into a cretin, a disgusting drunk. And Janis who was a charming drunk, was really put off by him. Well the more Janis rejected him, the more he loved it. This was a kind of match. Janis finally said to me, 'let's get out of here,' and we went to the band station wagon that she always drove. Jim came staggering over. He reached into the car and started to say something and she told him to fuck off. She wasn't interested anymore. Jim wasn't going to take no for an answer, though, and he reached into the car and grabbed Janis by the hair. Well, she picked up a bottle of Southern Comfort she had, reached out of the car, and

168

> wailed him on the head with it. He was out cold. The next day, I saw Jim in rehearsal and he said to me, 'What a great woman. She's terrific. Can I have her telephone number?' He was in love. Physical confrontation was his thing. He loved violence. (Riordan and Prochnicky, 173)

Riordan and Prochnicky also recount a typical incident that occurred with Pamela Courson. Frequently Pam and Jim argued about Pam wanting him to spend a quiet evening at home versus his wanting to party with friends. Often these arguments turned into knockdown, drag-out fights with their place getting smashed up despite all the careful work Pam had done in selecting furniture and decorating their apartment. This time after arguing:

> . . . Pam began screaming at him to leave and take his junk with him and started hurling books and dishes in a full on barrage. Morrison scrambled out the door and made it downstairs without getting hit. Once he was in the clear, Pam began heaving his stuff out the window and a huge pile of books, clothes and records was soon strewn about the front lawn . . . . The next day, when he had sobered up and she had calmed down, they went out on the lawn, picked everything up, and resumed their life as if nothing had happened (Riordan and

This appears to us to be a revealing example of the instability in all his relationships, i.e., the creation of chaos and the inability to experience even a close partner as real, whole, and satisfying for very long. Ever since childhood, Jim had reacted to his partners as a Jekyll and Hyde, sometimes gentle and charming, other times hostile, sadistic, and destructive. This behavior is typical of the disturbed object relations of someone who cannot help but split the people with whom he is trying to connect with into partial beings without "realness." Such a person is unable to maintain object constancy. Such relationships are a typical for those who live their life in the dead zone.

When The Music's Over

Before I sink, into the big sleep,
I want to hear, I want to hear,
The scream of the butterfly.

Twenty years after Jim Morrison's death, Densmore wrote that in the movie *The Doors*, actor Val Kilmer "miraculously re-created Jim." Densmore appears to have written his book as a modest attempt to comprehend his experience with *The Doors* and especially with the unpredictable, enraging, and enigmatic Morrison. Densmore's observation that the movie accurately captured the tormented but outrageous Morrison is consistent with the analysis we are offering. For most of his life, Morrison gave a whole new meaning to the terms self-destructive, confused, and desperate—symptoms of the borderline condition. Yet another instance in which art imitates life.

Like Janis, Jim had no true sense of himself as a person, man, or partner. Like her, he was a talented performer in search of a self, ultimately losing his struggle with the demons of the dead zone. And like her he acted provocatively, impulsively, and in accord with the need-fear dilemma (as described earlier, a primitive set of needs for nurturance and attachment counterbalanced by an equally primitive fear of closeness as threatening to one's own existence). He too functioned inconsistently, had no center, no focus and no capacity to self-soothe, and thus couldn't handle the ever present but incoherent dread. Both sought to commune with their audiences, but Jim's hostility and sadism dominated his relationships with the audience and with women. Janis looked for love among the living to escape the dead zone, while Jim sought pain and death for the same reason. Densmore discovered a never-released interview with Jim by a Lizzie Smith in which Jim says:

> Pain is meant to wake us up.
> People try to hide their pain.
> But they're wrong. Pain is
> something you carry, like a
> radio. You feel your strength in
> the experience of pain. . . . But
> people fear death even more
> than pain. It's strange that they
> fear death. Life hurts a lot more
> than death. At the point of
> death, the pain is over. I guess it
> is a friend. (Densmore, 196.

Jim believed that life hurt more than death because of the unbearable quality of the life he encountered in the dead zone, the only life he knew. Despairing and hopeless, those who live in the dead zone are so drained of emotional resources that they almost always live with the thought of suicide or experience suicidal ideation every day. Put differently, clinicians now refer to that experience as a weariness resulting from the struggle with constant existential despair and meaninglessness. Unable as he was to create the "internal objects" we all need in childhood, Morrison felt worse than dead. Riordan and Prochnicky:

> By the time of his death
> Morrison already knew that the

171

> real things tormenting him would not change with a new identity. He had a taste of that in Paris and discovered that it didn't matter where he lived, how famous he was, or what kind of work he did. The problem had to do with the way he was inside . . . . It was his inability to cope with the forces inside him that was destroying him. The tormenting echoes that drove him to the brink of madness on an almost daily basis (Riordan and Prochnicky, 471).

So even Jim at some point and at some level understood the futility of fighting the good fight against an enemy that was as yet undefined and extremely lethal. That he was able to perform at all, let alone in the high intensity light emanating from the rock music world, is remarkable. Regrettably, the great majority of those who experienced his performances never really understood his motivations that lay just beneath the surface.

Jim: After All

Jim could sadistically provoke because he could only experience others (or himself) as not quite real "partial objects." His emptiness and his inability to feel himself or others as real are two sides of the same condition. His provocativeness, his instigation of the audience, and his lifelong sadism should be viewed as desperate attempts to kindle a fire in others intense enough to warm his own bitter cold soul. If he could incite others to high enough levels of emotional intensity, then he might experience them—and thus himself—as real. He would escape from the dead zone on the feelings of life from those

172

whom he aroused to a fever pitch. His provocative behaviors toward his audiences and toward individuals, such as his obnoxious teasing of Janis on their only encounter, are less confusing when understood in this way. Strong reactions from others gave him moments of escape from the relentless dread of the dead zone.

Jim's life of intensely self-destructive abandon and hopelessness are familiar to clinicians who have worked with the identity diffused, emotionally isolative, or **detached** and internally barren patient. Based on our current clinical understanding of psychology and personality, we are now able to answer the same questions about Jim that we have already answered about Janis.

1. What was the matter with him? Why was his life such a chaotic affair?

The information we have gathered for this book, those observations of him made by his biographers, the portrayal of him in films, and his own words as recorded in personal interviews lead us to respond, as with Janis, to the two most frequently asked questions since his death.

To respond effectively, we must identify the characteristic features of Jim's' personality that permit us to offer our particular diagnosis. It is very clear to us now that he consistently exhibited:

- a clear pattern of instability in interpersonal relationships;
- an unstable and vague self-image and identity;
- shifting and unpredictable moods;
- a poor control of impulses and emotions
  beginning in early adulthood and evident in a
  variety of contexts.
- a pervasive feeling of emptiness/deadness

This description happens to be consistent with the same diagnosis we believe to have been the case for Janis: *the Borderline Personality Disorder* as defined by the *Diagnostic and Statistical Manual of the American Psychiatric Association*

173

(DSM-IV, see appendix 2).

Thus, in modern clinical terms, the response to the first question is that Jim was increasingly incapacitated by a personality disorder that was little known or understood at that time. His chaotic life, like Janis's, may now be understood as having resulted from that disorder. Typically, in their desperation to escape the inner feelings of tension and dread, most *detached type* borderline personalities like Jim tend to cut a complicated and troublesome life path strewn with debris. As mentioned earlier, many of the people we read about in the daily news and about whom we wonder, "How could they do that?" or "What a stupid thing to do?" or "Why would anyone act that way?" may well be struggling with borderline disorders.

2. How did he die? Did he kill himself?

We obviously can never know for certain. Pamela Courson arranged for his burial in Pere Lachaise cemetery in Paris before his death was made public. All the evidence and the understanding of his borderline condition make it difficult to determine whether he deliberately killed himself or was simply another unlucky drug user. As we have already discussed, however, the reason why he took drugs is pertinent: to help him manage a despair and an unbearable inner tension which were laying waste to his emotional life.

If his death, (and Janis'), was not a consciously intentional suicide, it nevertheless came as a consequence of engaging in behaviors aimed at escaping the inner emotional barrenness of life. In a sense, Jim and Janis are examples of one kind of deadly conflict waged for the soul of a person, a conflict Karl Menninger described almost three decades ago in his book, *Man Against Himself.*

What Menniger concludes is that inexplicable external behaviors are the result of struggles with untamed, internal, and aggressive forces present in all humans. These self-destructive and aggressive forces can be avoided only if one has achieved some form of mental health via psychological mechanisms such as sublimation, instinctual regulation, and personality integration, which develop from at least a "good enough environment," along with a temperament low in vulnerability to ordinary childhood stress (good protoplasm).

3. How was he different if at all from the many other public figures who died prematurely by their own hand?

It is now safe to assert that there are other public figures who were suffering then, as others are now, with one of the many types of borderline condition. Remember that clinicians at present are certain enough of the borderline profiles that they can easily point to Zelda Fitzgerald and Marilyn Monroe as possible borderline types. Monroe was treated for years by the well-known and highly regarded psychoanalyst, Ralph Greenson. Monroe's biographers record chronic behaviors that are consistent with what we know today to be borderline conditions. In her case, like Janis and Jim's, clinical psychiatry had not yet framed the outlines of the condition; and thus these celebrities were to find no relief in therapy, no relief from the dread.

So what is clear is that Janis and Jim were unlike most public figures who die by their own hand. Many borderline patients die indirectly as an unintended outcome of the impulsivity characteristic of borderline conditions, and are typically unable to become very public figures. Generally, a moderate-to-severe borderline condition makes it difficult for someone to achieve at all, except perhaps when public recognition is achieved by sensational behaviors.

4. What difference does this information make?

This modern understanding of the borderline condition that affected Janis and Jim can alert us to the symptoms of the condition and its recognizable consequences. We believe that there are more lives at stake here than entertainers. By casting our eye on the more visible and more well known cases of borderlines, we hope to increase the probability that others suffering from the same condition will be diagnosed and treated. For as it now stands, there are many reasons why the behavior of borderlines escapes serious scrutiny from the public.

In Jim's case, his outrageous and often sadistic behaviors could easily dissuade others from empathizing with him, from looking any closer than they had to. So his anguish, like Janis's, poured out of him in poetry and song, predictably overwhelming his audience with the depth of his despair. His audiences might have understandably been moved, but what they didn't and couldn't appreciate was how utterly desperate his actions were and how terror-filled were his lyrics. The real meaning of his provocative, chaotic activities becomes comprehensible only as an evermore frantic attempt to avoid falling further into the nightmare, into the dead zone.

Like Janis, Jim was impulse-ridden, wracked by a wretched hunger for human attachments, yet unable to be satisfied or soothed by them. He possessed no inner core, or sense of himself, and therefore simply could not "connect" with anyone. His agony was poignantly revealed in the cacophony of words and images he brought onto the stage, unconsciously trying to communicate his experience of the "nameless dread." It was an experience few others could know unless they were similarly trapped. We are convinced that part of his hold on audiences had to do with the way his rage and protest against the dead zone, as revealed in his words and actions, reached into the unnamed and darkest corner of the souls who heard him.

Chapter Six: Reflections on Destiny—Jim

"I wish clean death would come to me"

Joyce McDougall, the French psychoanalyst who has worked extensively with creative people of all types including those in the performing arts, believes that truly creative acts come not from whatever psychopathology an artist might have but from the healthiest part of the artist's personality. Like Janis, Jim was more than the sum of his psychological disturbances. Certainly the signs and symptoms of Jim Morrison's pathology covered the rock landscape. Nevertheless, his vocalizations, charisma, stage presence, songs, and some of his poetry emerged from the healthier elements in Jim's personality and did not derive from his borderline condition. The tragedy was that the real promise of Jim Morrison was unrealized at the time of his death.

Our contention is that Jim's reaction to a lifelong residency in the dead zone is the most reasonable explanation for his preoccupation with mystical ideas, madness, pain, chaos, and death. He used his considerable intellect to try to batter his way out, and for the same reason was drawn to the writings of his intellectual mentors, Rimbaud, Blake, Nietzsche, and Kafka. They seemed to whisper in his ear: defy all conventional logic, stir up the pot, test all limits, flirt with the very edge of experience and beyond. Wasn't it Rimbaud who glorified madness, Blake who urged an alteration of perception, and Kafka who told of alienation from the self? Wasn't it Nietzsche who talked of supermen and who said, "the last Christian died on the cross"? These were the intellectual ideas that informed Morrison's behavior.

Those who would glorify Jim's aberrant, outrageous, and inane behaviors as the wellsprings of his creative process misunderstand him. The idea that Jim's behavior was the result of an intellectual journey of any kind is insupportable. Instead, his search for ways out of the dead zone caused him, like so many others, to seek the excitement of intense experiences, to escape the emptiness and inner chaos, and along the way he found the intellectual rationalization for his actions. That he was able to use his readings and philosophical explorations to create new combinations of words and themes in music and poetry is a tribute to his intelligence and the healthy part of him. His was creative *in spite* of his life in the dead zone, not because of it.

In *No One Here Gets Out Alive,* Hopkins and Sugerman describe Jim's manipulation of the audience, teasing and waiting until they became restless and angry at his doing nothing, just standing in a trance, as he often did:

> It's like watching a mural . . .
> There's movement and then it's
> frozen. I like to see just how
> long they can stand it, and when
> they're about to crack, I let go
> (Hopkins and Sugerman, 134).

Morrison was then asked about what he would do if the crowd went berserk and rushed the stage like they were going to kill him. He cited theories about the sexual neuroses of crowds and then said:

> I always know exactly when to
> do it. That excites people. You
> know what happens. They get
> frightened, and fear is very
> exciting. People like to get
> scared. It's exactly like the
> moment before you have an
> orgasm. Everybody wants that.
> It's a peaking experience
> (Riordan and Prochnicky 1991,
> 136).

Of course, not everybody is like that, seeking the ultimate thrill in defying danger or death. Indeed, it appears his fans understood very little of the real motivations for his antics.

As he was busy defying, Jim accumulated quite an arrest record in the brief period of his adult life. FBI records show him to have been arrested at least ten times between 1963 and 1969 on such charges as drunk driving, lewd and lascivious behavior, battery, driving without a license, and interference with the flight of an aircraft (Riordan and Prochnicky, 346-347). Consider how Jim's life might have turned out if a judge, given this record, had ordered him to undertake individual psychotherapy for alcohol abuse while he was on probation.

Though there is little reason to believe that he would have sought such help, Riordan and Prochnicky report that Jim, on the urging of Pamela Courson's father, once had a few sessions with a psychiatrist (Riordan and Prochnicky, 172). However, he strung the psychiatrist along with a stream of intellectual and philosophical gibberish, ending the sessions abruptly. Jim was just playing with the psychiatrist and quickly became bored with him. Thus simply forcing Jim into treatment with a competent therapist trained in borderline psychopathology may or may not have made a difference. Although Jim did not permit any serious analysis of his behavior and personality, we can offer an account of how a session with Jim *might* have been, with the aid of developments in modern clinical psychoanalysis.

Imagine then, a reluctant Jim Morrison ordered into psychotherapy, a common experience these days. The time is November, 1970. Following Jimi Hendricks by two weeks, Janis Joplin had died of complications following an injection of heroin. Jim is aware that he is slipping into despair, voicing his concern that he doesn't know who he is. The excitement of performing and inciting people isn't enough to quiet the demons anymore. At best the emptiness has become more dreadful. Initially his first line of defense—alcohol—has ceased to numb the pain of the emptiness. He is thinking of getting away, thinking again of doing more work on his poetry. In his mind, Paris offers him hope as he plans to leave the *Doors*. Janis's death bothers him. He has his own lingering preoccupation with death. What follows are segments of several sessions conducted across many months in late 1970 and early 1971.

He reacts to psychotherapy with disdain and scorn, but he aches deep in his porous self-core and harbors a vague, unconscious hope that something or someone might pull him up from the void.

Session 1:

The first appointment occurs in late November, 1970. His long suffering girlfriend, Pam, is to leave for Paris in February of 1971 and it is expected that he would follow her in April. The other members of the *Doors* had sensed Jim's restlessness and uncertainty about the future. So when he is ordered into treatment they are hopeful.

Jim shows up ten minutes late for the first appointment, overweight and bearded. I greet him. He looks around as he enters the room, avoids a handshake and sits without a word, waiting for me to start. He presents as cynical and detached, and has a strange trance-like expression on his face, similar to the way he looks in the publicity pictures of him. He does not rush in to engage. I begin by explaining what I have been told about him:

GAF: My understanding is that you have been in some difficulty with the law. The probation officer told me you have been arrested on a number of occasions for various offenses, for driving while intoxicated and for lascivious behavior. In this last instance the judge ordered you to try six sessions of therapy as a condition of probation.

Jim: Yeah. *(Looking bored, he is dressed in tight black leather pants and a loose, white linen. His face is drawn, perhaps from drugs or alcohol, and he is overweight. His dark, curly hair is rather unkempt. Slumped in his chair, leg sprawled, Jim doesn't look much like the young lion in the famous poster of him.)*

GAF: Can you enlighten me a bit about all this?

Jim: *(He is looking mildly annoyed and as if he is trying to decide whether to bother, but he finally does, speaking slowly and sarcastically without intonation.)* The uptight little man judge thinks he knows what he's doing but he doesn't. He doesn't get what it's all about and neither do you. What really matters isn't what he thinks matters, and he can't figure it out.

It's not his fault he can't understand. He's hopelessly out of touch so he can't take it all in. *(Jim's intellectual arrogance is the by-product of using his mind to defend against the dread which always grips him.)*

GAF: How do you mean 'what really matters?'

Jim: *(Looking disinterested and speaking in monotone)* I'm not interested in this game . . . in your mindless shrink games. There's no point talking to you. You want to get into my mind, do your thing. Figure out why I do what I do. It's pointless. You can't. *(Jim so far, has used words/phrases such as, "can't figure it out," can't understand," "hopeless," and "pointless." The words used by a patient are important in that they often apply elsewhere in his/her psychology. Here I begin to wonder if Jim is feeling hopeless, too. I make a mental note of this and the possibility that his history of drug and alcohol abuse is an attempt at self-medication.)*

GAF: Well, maybe we could try anyway.

Jim: Maybe. (*Looking at me out of the corner of his eye, one brow raised*) But you don't seem any smarter than the judge. Stuck here in your dull little world.

GAF: (*Ignoring the hostility for now and bringing in the reality of his situation*) Well, it seems that the court is requiring that you be in therapy somewhere until your probation is up. So as long as you're here, maybe we can both learn something instead of staring at each other for fifty minutes.

Jim: Yeah . . . maybe. So what are you, Freudian . . . Adlerian . . .

Jungian? *(Drifting off, he responds laconically. I get little suspicious that he might be high. His awareness of Freud, Adler, and Jung reflect his reported familiarity with some psychoanalytic literature)*.

GAF: Is it important to you which?

Jim: No, it doesn't matter.

GAF: What does matter?

Jim: *(Speaking softly, slowly and as if to himself)* Pain matters, chaos matters, death matters, sex matters, the senses matter, experiences matter . . . fear matters . . . the only realities.

GAF: Sounds a bit morbid.

Jim: *(Again, slowly and softly. I believe now that he has had a few drinks)* I knew you wouldn't dig it. You've never lived on the edge . . . try to see hell, touch the sky.

185

GAF: Living on the edge of physical experience?

Jim: That's where it is, man, everything else is illusion, boring. Danger is real. Death is the ultimate gig.

GAF: Does this view of life affect your work? *(I am unfamiliar with the Doors.)*

Jim: Of course. We're sexual politicians. We get people off, move them over the edge into orgasm. If you're Freudian you must have read Norman Brown— you know about man's repression by society. *(Smiles broadly.)* I'm kind of like you . . . a healer, a shaman, treating the fucked up, the repressed. But I use music and poetry to help to liberate people. I'm able to free them from their neuroses, get them beyond the blinders and the rules. I excite them, arouse their anger and pain . . .

their sexuality, to get to their impulses. *(Jim is becoming more verbal, but his manner is still bland and low key.)*

GAF: *(I remain silent while Jim is beginning to become a bit relaxed and expansive. Perhaps he is taking the opportunity to espouse his views. Still, at times he seems distracted. There is a slight smirk on his face as he speaks.)*

Jim: Of course, the judge and the cops and the lawyers are just as fucked up as everybody else, they just don't know it. I want every experience to try and go beyond the ordinary . . . the rules . . . the limits imposed by society. You can't get anywhere until you get past the shit and sharpen your senses . . . to touch the boundaries of existence. Even death, it's the ultimate experience and I don't want to go out unconscious and miss it. *(A brief silence)* Jimi Hendricks and Janis have already checked out but the word is that they were high. Not me, I won't be. Death is a door, something to go through and be transformed, like the shaman . . . . *(After a pause, he shifts emotionally, as if in slow motion.)* Have you read Rimbaud or Blake or Poe or Kafka? They understood.

GAF: How long have you been thinking about checking out?

Jim: Always. The final boundary. People are afraid, they don't understand that death is freedom. You don't understand either, do you? *(Condescending, Jim is now warming up a bit and appears slightly more alert.)* It's too bad, you should understand. Freud had a bit of it . . . a glimmer. He knew that civilized man has been deprived of his impulses and senses . . . that . . . that all real experience, all of man's instincts and drives have been encased in the cement of culture and society. That the raw experience of life is stifled, smothered in rules, commandments, in the demand for order. The only way is back to the subconscious, by becoming aware of all that has been pushed out of our immediate consciousness by civilization. And I know there is one way to get there—by breaking the hold reality has on us, by experiencing everything, breaking through to disorder and the primacy of the senses. Rimbaud knew—sanity through insanity. Blake knew— the doors between the known and the unknown. *(Jim's superior intelligence is obvious and he is now showing an impressive grasp of certain philosophical and psychological ideas, such as the question Freud raised about civilization being the cause of neurotic conflict in man, i.e., civilization fosters the rules that repress most of man's natural instincts. But Jim distorts these ideas to justify his behavior, which is really the result of his struggle with the dead zone.)*

GAF: Are you saying that you get drunk to experience life more fully? Seems to me that being drunk is more like a barrier to fully experiencing anything. Alcohol doesn't expand the senses, it clouds them. *(I've decided to challenge him and create just a little cognitive dissonance around his intellectualizing.)*

Jim: No. No. *(Jim reacts to my challenge. Energized, he sits up and leans forward to engage me more fully. He obviously wants to*

explain himself now.)
Everything I do is to free me up. I want to experience everything more vividly, more intensely. Huxley used mescaline to expand his consciousness. I want to know things one can't know without changing the way our senses work—to experience the unknown, to find what 's meaningful. I've always thought about it. Alcohol is just a part of the trip, and part of stirring things up.

GAF: Could there be other reasons for your search for meaning and experience?

Jim: What do you mean? *(his voice indicating he's becoming annoyed at my probing question)*

GAF: Well, what are existence and experience like for you without expanding the senses?

Jim: Painful . . . death is . . .

really a friend because life is pain. Like standing on the down slope of some dark, angry void. *(He is staring slightly now. I'm trying to evaluate his state of mind.)*

GAF: Dark, angry void?

Jim: Yeah . . . .*(He shifts mood again and becomes hostile, and his narcissism also appears more blatantly.)* What's the matter, can't Freud explain someone like me, or am I just too much for *you*?

GAF: *(Although I cannot know at this point what is going on with Jim, I would tend to address his hostility. And the phrase angry void catches my attention. It may be the poetic language of an intellectual who is depressed, or the words of a cynic. Or maybe neither.)* Maybe you're concerned that I won't be able to explain you?

(I believe he means help him). And maybe that scares you and makes you angry? That there may be no help for the pain?

Jim: *(First he looks away angry and disgusted. Then he leans forward and glares at me.)* What a fucking asshole. You don't jerk off enough. You need to get rid of the bullshit and get more pussy. Your mind is dead from too much Freud and too little action. Get fucked. *(Jim's mini-tirade is somewhat moderated by his uncertainty regarding what happens in a therapy session, and by his probation. But I touched a nerve, one very close to his despair.)*

GAF: *(I give him a questioning look, meant to ask non-verbally, "what was that all about?". My expectation is that he will be forthcoming once he sees that I'm not intimidated or made angry by his tirade.)* What just happened?

Jim: You pissed me off. You think you know something. But you don't. You're just playing shrink games. *(Jim is slowly becoming less agitated and seems to settle back a bit in the chair.)*

GAF: Mmm. You thought my question was part of a game?

Jim: Look, I told you all this doesn't matter. I'm only here because of that cretin of a judge. *(now sullen)*

GAF: Well, this form of therapy is non-coercive, and the patient comes to explore what things mean to him, why he is self-defeating or what his conflicts are all about—why he is anxious or depressed or angry. They are motivated by the desire to understand. People come to lower their misery level. *(I attempt a little educating here).*

Jim: You and I are in different worlds. You think everybody's neurotic, and you try to analyze them. I see everybody as fucked. Fucked by all the bullshit that I try to break down. So . . . we have nothing in common. You don't get it. You don't understand! (Angrily *shaking his head)*

GAF: *(I am looking to capture his interest by touching on his emotional stress and intellectual arrogance.)* I usually understand anguish, despair, pain, hopelessness, anxiety. Maybe there's more to your search than you realize.

Jim: What the fuck are you talking about?

GAF: You mentioned that life is pain, a 'dark angry void.' Is that how it is

195

for you personally? Or was that a rhetorical— *(He cuts me off)*

Jim: So! That's just the way life is. (*Annoyed and dismissive*)

GAF: *(Trying again)* For you too?

Jim: For everybody. Only some don't know it, they're too numb to it and only know the rules. (*appears disgusted*)

GAF: Well. How is it for you to feel that angry void?

Jim: *(Thinking for a moment, he seems to find the question interesting.)* I use it. I make it work for me, and people use me to come alive instead of staying repressed and bored. *(Jim is slowly being drawn into a philosophical discussion, but his inner feelings are there behind the words).*

GAF: So you make them feel

alive. Just how do you do that?

Jim: By working on them, teasing, taunting . . . and then the music pulls them over the edge and they lose it . . . I know just how to do it, to tease it out. *(He's appears proud of his philosophy here, but I find his pose nonetheless unconvincing, leaving me with the impression that he doesn't really believe it.)*

GAF: So you're not feeling repressed and bored when you're doing that for them?

Jim: *(Shakes head)* That's right. It's like magic. Like the shaman who channels everything through himself and takes on their impulses and anger. *(Here maybe is a touch of the Christian belief about Christ taking on the sins of man—perhaps a bit of Jim's mysticism and grandiosity.)*

GAF: How are you feeling
when you're not taking
on the impulses and
anger of others? Are
you feeling the way
they do?

Jim: Yeah. I know how they
feel and they know I do,
so they respond to me.

GAF: So you know how they
feel. You have the same
angry void they do.
What is it really like for
you?

Jim: *(He is angry again. My
question challenges his
attempts to maintain an
intellectual/mystical
aura around his
feelings so as to keep
them controlled. Jim is
very smart and isn't
going to be easily led to
talk about himself at
this level.)* Are we
finished for today? This
is going nowhere. It's
pathetic that you sit
there thinking you can
understand me when
you're stuck with this
crap job and play these
games. You're blind

and don't know it. *(Agitated, he turns away from me in his chair, a deep frown on his face.)*

GAF: Perhaps, but it surprises me that you seem to find my question so problematic. *(I continue here to stay on the subject of his angry feeling. Eventually he might find my question harder to ignore.)*

Jim: *(He reacts coolly and with obvious agitation.)* It's no problem. But we have no common language. You won't get it, and I'm in no mood to try to fill you in. So . . . I have to go.

GAF: Maybe we can try again next time. *(He leaves without further comment).*

Not an unusual session for this type of patient who can be sullen, arrogant, and intellectual. He nurses his pain with complex ideas and philosophy. Because he is so intelligent he can challenge and evade with perspectives and attitudes that the therapist might find interesting and therefore distracting.

Jim misses the second session and arrives for the third ten

minutes late, disconnected and aloof.

Session 3.

Jim: I can only stay for ten minutes . . . I have a rehearsal.

GAF: Well, ten minutes won't be helpful to you, so we should reschedule.

Jim: Okay. See you later. *(He leaves)*

Session 4.

Jim's oppositional tendencies are pronounced. He would continue to avoid and evade the sessions until his probation was over, but the probation officer pulls him in and he arrives for the next session on time. He is annoyed and recalcitrant. We spar again, but he does begin to ease up on his negativity because he is still feeling the dread of the dead zone.

Jim: That little fuck *(the probation officer)* is a pathetic, mindless robot.

GAF: He hassled you?

Jim: Yeah. Checked up on my schedule and found out I missed a session. Then he did his big man speech about, 'you have to work with me Jim. We can work this out but you've gotta give me some cooperation.' The little fuck . . . .

GAF: Mmmn. Well. Maybe we can use the time. You're a man with some interesting ideas and convictions. *(I'm appealing to his intellectual vanity).*

Jim: Yeah . . . maybe. Go ahead, ask what you want. *(Jim is less agitated with me than in the first session, at least for now.)*

GAF: It's not what I want, it's what you feel about yourself and your life and how we might together find a new way of looking at things. That's what therapy offers. We can learn something and maybe break through the confusion.

Jim: Yeah? What things? What confusion? I'm not the one who's confused. (*Annoyed, he scowls at me.*)

GAF: I meant the confusion between us. It's unclear to me, for example, just what your feelings about life and death are all about.

Jim: I told you what matters. Pain, sex, experiences, and death. (*Impatiently*)

GAF: It would help to know how you've come to this view.

Jim: It's obvious isn't it. Look around at people and how stiff and scared and angry they are. Their all looking for a peak experience, to let loose, and they don't know how.

GAF: How can you be sure that people feel that way?

Jim: I read it in their faces . . . in their uptight faces.

GAF: Is it possible that you feel scared and angry, too, and that when you

look at them you see the
reflection of your own
feelings in their faces?
*(I'm confronting him
once again, suggesting
that Jim could be
projecting his own
anxieties onto others.)*

Jim: What?   *(Disdainfully)*
You can't use that
shrink shit on me. I'm
seeking the very things
that frighten them—
letting go, busting out. I
don't project onto them,
I entice and instigate. I
liberate them. *(Jim is
laid back in the chair,
becoming calmer as he
speaks; he is feeling
more sure of himself as
he uses his intelligence
to hide his demons.)*

GAF: What is it like for you
to entice and instigate?

Jim: What do you mean?

GAF: What are you feeling
when you entice and
instigate . . . and
liberate them?
*(I ask about his
intentions here because
Jim does not seem to be*

interested in his audiences merely to promote his career, as someone driven purely by the quest for glory, so I'm hoping to push him to explore his real motives.)

Jim: *(Ponders the question.)* I don't know. It's just the way I am. What difference does it make?

GAF: Well, you know, I was wondering what you might be experiencing when you're performing.

Jim: It's a high, a peak experience. At least it used to be, but it's not like that now. I think that uhh, I'm getting tired. I'm going to move on, maybe publish more of my poetry. (*Then as an afterthought*) I plan to join Pamela in Paris in a few months.

GAF: You're leaving your band?

Jim: Yeah, after the next

tour.

GAF: Do I understand you correctly, that you no longer feel the same satisfaction on stage as you once did?

Jim: Yeah, that's right. *(This is the first time Jim has made a direct comment about his personal feelings rather than an intellectual/philosophical argument.)*

GAF: Could you tell me more about what's changed?

Jim: I don't know, things are just different. It's as if none of it matters anymore. I've got to move on, experience everything and get my thoughts together. Work on my poetry. The poets are the only truly tuned in people. They move along the fault lines of life, they meet the chaos and pain head on . . . . *(Jim is rambling a bit— the closest he will get to 'free associating' in therapy.)*

GAF: You've mentioned the pain of life a few times now. You experience life as painful?

Jim: Yes . . . so? Doesn't everybody? *(Jim, like others living in the dead zone, can't really describe the experience of the dead zone. He tends to project his anxiety onto the world.)*

GAF: Not the way you describe it. How is it so painful for you?

Jim: *(Stares at me for a while. Jim's anger and hostility of the first session are absent now and he sighs, sits back in a more relaxed fashion, and seems to be pondering my question. For a moment I wonder if he is gaining some interest in the therapy. I am wrong.)* You still haven't figured out what I'm talking about. You're a rather disappointing example of your profession. Are you typical? How could

206

you possibly help anyone? You're not smart enough, and you're not experienced enough. *(Jim is speaking slowly and quietly, and in a scornful voice. My question clearly upset him.)*

GAF: My question angers you?

Jim: You're just another flunky doing what you've been trained to do by an ossified discipline and those who fear their own natural instincts. You try to inhibit those who aren't afraid, who seek the truth . . . the poets, for example. What kind of Freudian are you anyway? What kind of training and education did you have that left you so uncomprehending? I would've expected you to appreciate the need for releasing pent-up impulses. Repressing leaves you soft-headed and frustrated. So, why are you so dense?

GAF: You mentioned Freud several times, and seem to have more than a cursory grasp of his ideas. Are you rejecting his concept that we're all moved more by unconscious motives than conscious ones? After all, repression is a defense based on the idea of the unconscious. Or are you saying your motives aren't mostly unconscious like the rest of us? *(I am directly challenging Jim. I have not been able to move him into examining his behavior or to reflect on his repeated angry or defensive reactions to all questions about his personal feelings. His last reaction seems to have been triggered by my effort to focus him on pain in a more personal way. So the challenge is a bit of a risk but is intended to upset his defensive adjustment of projecting and intellectualizing his painful feelings.)*

Jim: See, you're off course again. I know that everything really important is unconscious. Our motives are unconscious. That's why I've been exploring my unconscious for as long as I can remember. And the unconscious is where you find the chaos, the sensuality, and sexuality—really find the essence of life. No rules, no restrictions, no bullshit. It's being, without inhibiting the senses, the inhibition that makes life painful and death friendly. I'm surprised that you find this so difficult to figure out. I don't think I've misjudged you. You can't get it because you're blinded by the game plan of a society that alienates you from yourself. *(Jim's intelligence once again helps him to avoid the implications of my questioning. Here is a good example of how a strength and intelligence can be used to defend against the emergence of threatening but largely unconscious feelings e.g., dread and despair.)*

GAF: *(I try again).* I am still puzzled by your reluctance to discuss the pain you mention at a more personal level, as readily as you do at the level of the group and in society. Especially if you maintain, as you do, that you are in touch with your own unconscious.

Jim: You want to know more about pain? Is the concept of pain so hard to understand? Everybody's in pain.

GAF: Well, pain is a more general word for discomfort of some kind, but it's nonspecific. If you're talking about psychological pain, then there are many possibilities — apprehension, worry, anxiety, dread as one continuum for example. Or sadness, grief, depression, despair as another, or agitation, irritability, anger, rage as a third. These can be part of psychological pain, and I can't figure out from what you've told me whether or not in your case any or all of these are involved.

Jim: What difference does it make? It's all the same thing man, can't you see that? Haven't you read Sartre and the existentialists? It's about alienation and about a kind of nonexistence, of nothingness. No feelings . . . no sensation . . . no meaning, no hope.

GAF: No feeling and no hope. Are those your feelings, too?

Jim: Yeah, like almost

everybody else, except most don't even know that they're alienated from themselves. They blindly accept the repression of society and never get beyond it.

GAF: You see the restrictions of society and its rules as the cause of your feelings of hopelessness. Could there be other causes?

Jim: What do you mean? *(An opening, maybe. Jim might be willing to entertain the idea that some of his pain is independent of society.)*

GAF: Well, we haven't discussed your background. Perhaps some of those feelings stem from early experiences. *(At this point, I have yet to realize that Jim may be living in the dead zone. So I'm looking to explore any childhood precipitants of pain.)*

Jim: What early experiences?

GAF: Any that may have shaped your feelings about life and yourself. Since you're familiar with Freud you know that he felt like Wadsworth, that 'the child is father to the man.' We're all shaped by our history. Your relationship with your parents, for example.

Jim: My parents are dead.

GAF: Oh, then I was given an incorrect summary by the probation officer. He indicated that your parents live in Florida, and that your dad is an admiral in the navy. The officer talked to the authorities in Florida where you apparently had a run-in with the law last year.

Jim: Yeah, that's right. But they're dead to me.

GAF: How did you come to feel this way?

Jim: They're just not

213

important, that's all.
Let's just move on . . . .

This session is illustrative of the difficulties facing any therapist trying to conduct a session with an unwilling patient. Jim would present problems for any therapist. The first problem is that he is not interested in therapy. A second problem is his unwillingness to reflect on his inner world, preferring instead to project his discomforts onto others. And third, he is unable to acknowledge his background and provide the historical context for his character and behavior. And finally, he uses his intelligence to challenge the therapist's sense of competence and to attack. But despite these problems, the therapist has one ally—Jim's desire to end his own misery. His intelligence cannot fully compensate for the way his underlying pathology distorts his view of things. By bringing distortions into sharp relief and showing a willingness to explore nonjudgmentally the meaning of behavior and feelings, the therapist can offer hope to the patient. Jim has stayed in session twice, and the hope is that he is starting to feel the beginnings of trust and to hope for relief from the pain.

Jim comes for the fifth session. He is a few minutes late but exhibits none of the arrogant, oppositional behavior of the other sessions. Instead he is milder in manner and even looks a bit depressed. He looks at me expectantly.

Session 5.

Jim: *Jim is dressed in black, looking very tired, almost defeated.*)
So what do we talk about today?

GAF: Well, how have things gone for you this week?

214

Jim: I don't know. I'm just tired of it all. Nothing feels good. So what do you make of that? *(Jim may be feeling the chaos and emptiness of the dead zone now. Perhaps he's hoping I can help somehow, yet, at the same time he feels the despair that is always with him. But at this point, I cannot diagnose the cause of his despair.)*

GAF: It makes me wonder about what could be going on. In spite of your success, you feel tired and dissatisfied.

Jim: *(He looks at me, apparently trying to decide whether to respond to my comment or to ignore it. He sits silently for a few moments and then with a look that appears to be a mixture of anticipation and disdain, he seems ready to put down whatever I say, yet part of him is still hopeful.)* Yeah,

215

well, you're the shrink.
What do your books
say?

GAF: Sometimes feeling tired
and nothing feeling
good are symptoms of
depression. Sometimes
they are symptoms of
an internal conflict as in
Pogo's famous line 'we
have met the enemy and
he is us.' We need a
little more detail about
these symptoms before
we can make sense of
them.

Jim: Detail? Like what? *(Jim
is reluctantly drawn in
by what is left of hope
in him. But that hope is
but a distant flicker of
light.)*

GAF: Like how you feel in
different settings, how
you feel about your
work, how are your
intimate relationships.
Freud, when asked
about what constituted
emotional health
supposedly said, the
ability 'to love and to
work.' Are you able to
love and to work, and to

be gratified?

Jim: Huh! You mean fuck and write? Yeah. So?

GAF: Maybe there's more to it. Fucking is not loving. And you say that you're not feeling very good, that you feel miserable. Can you elaborate?

Jim: Elaborate what? I'm tired and fed up. The whole scene has become boring and meaningless. I need to get away, work on my poetry. *(Jim trails off. After a few moments he returns to his lament, in a vague, mournful voice.)* I don't feel the excitement anymore. The whole thing is . . . irrelevant. I . . . need to find . . . I don't know what I want to do. Don't even know who I am, what I want. Have you ever read Camus' novel *The Stranger*. I know that guy, I know where he's coming from. Problem is, he's all fucked up. *(I found this to be a remarkable admission from Jim considering his talk in previous sessions. He stares out the window.)*

GAF: *(I am alerted by this last comment about The Stranger. The character in Camus' book is a good example of someone living in the dead zone.)* That guy is detached and alienated from himself and from life. Is that how you feel?

Jim: That's right. He can't get into it. There's nothing there or anywhere that makes any difference to him. He can't find a way to really experience the reality behind the empty actions of the blind and gullible masses. So he has no hope.

GAF: You're feeling hopeless then?

Jim: You could say that. *(Still in a contemplative mood.)* What would justify hope? Nothing in

218

life is hopeful because the meaning of existence is hidden behind the conventions of civilization. *(Jim falls into his intellectual defenses now.)* Action's better than inaction, chaos is better than order, sex is better than chastity, death is better than life. I've told you all this. Only people who don't comprehend this can fool themselves into being hopeful.

GAF: *(Challenging Jim directly here would only harden his defenses. Instead, I try to increase trust and form an alliance with Jim by staying focused on his subjective experience of himself and life. So I will ask him how he feels about the way he feels.)* It must be very hard to walk around without hope. How is it for you to feel the way you do?

Jim: *(Jim readily understands this question. He looks up*

and becomes more intense as he describes himself.) It gives me a sense of power. I'm not stopped by common fears. Having no belief in the ordinary, I can take on anything, challenge all the petty bullshit, live on the edge, closer to the boundary between smothering social mores and the liberating qualities of sex, drugs, and death. Christ had a piece of it. Lose yourself to find yourself.

GAF: Uh huh. You've resigned yourself to hopelessness and find yourself free to defy the world. You have no fear because you have no hope.

Jim: That's right . . . you're finally getting it.

(But *Jim does not strike me as feeling good about his success in helping me to "finally get it." He looks tormented still.*)

GAF: What if you're wrong?

Jim: What are you talking about?

GAF: What if your conclusions about why you feel hopeless are wrong? What if the reasons for your agitation and despair are not what you believe them to be?

Jim: Yeah . . . okay . . . What's your theory? *Jim's voice signals to me that while he doesn't dare let hope enter into his life, he does hope.)*

GAF: *(I will try to capture his interest again as he seems ready to consider alternatives to his views. I am now aware that he may be living in the dead zone. I will try to use Camus' The Stranger to make it easier for Jim to consider that he may also feel the dead zone.)* You say you feel like the stranger? From my point of view, the

221

stranger was alienated from himself and all others as well. He was living with an existential despair that was always part of him, a sense of nothingness that did not derive from the suppression of his instincts and senses, but from unknown developmental glitches in his identity formation and in his ability to attach to others. He would have felt this way as long as he could recall. For example, questioning reality, seeking to be aroused or excited in , order to escape the nothingness, or to quiet the dread and agitation that are part of the despair. Is that true for you? That you've always felt this way? *(I'm checking a hypothesis by using Camus' character).*

Jim: Yeah . . . .

GAF: And you find that excitement changes your experience of the nothingness?

222

Jim: Yeah, maybe.

GAF: Could it be that your insistence on action, sensation, sex, and intense experiences are your way of gaining relief from the nothingness and the inner agitation?

Jim: *(Jim reflects on these ideas and his intelligence helps him here. But at the same time he is oppositional, narcissistic, and hostile, therefore unpredictable. But now he is quiet.)* Maybe . . . maybe.

GAF: If you recall, *The Stranger* was unmoved by the death of his mother. Even committing murder left him without feeling of any kind. So intense experiences didn't help him. Do I understand you correctly, that you might be feeling that way?

Jim: Yeah . . . maybe. Not a bad theory, but . . .

.(Jim remains attentive, pensive and slightly skeptical. But he is still listening.)

GAF: Have you felt this way, this nothingness, as long as you can remember?

Jim: Yeah, *(Jim's looking more despondent as we talk. Then, after some time passes, Jim looks at me expectantly)*. So what about it? Your theory's not bad. But it's not new. I've known that all along. What difference does it make? Are you talking about a kind of, uh, developmental glitch? *(Notice how Jim has just accepted an alternative way of explaining his troubles by appropriating it as his own and as not new. His challenge to me, "What difference does it make?" is offered in the hope that I might be able to help without him asking for it.)*

GAF: Well, maybe we can

explore it together, maybe find ways to ease up the agitation and soften the nothingness. We might find some answers for the alienation. It depends on understanding your experiences better than we do.

Jim: Yeah . . . understanding what?

GAF: Well, for example, can you get hold of your inner state of feeling when you are not performing, not drinking, and not taking drugs? Can you describe what it's like to be you under ordinary circumstances?

Jim: I don't know, maybe. It's just like the way things are, like boring, meaningless. *(long silence)* I don't know.

GAF: Boring and agitating at the same time?

Jim: Yeah. And unreal. *(Here again is the dead*

zone paradox. The person is feeling empty and emotionally turbulent at the same time, i.e., bored and agitated.)

GAF: Unreal?

Jim: Yeah . . . unreal. You know, like when you feel as if . . . as though you're a mechanical man, or maybe like you're acting in a play and not really there. As though everything was a dream, like you were ethereal . . . amorphous . . . like you're just a two-dimensional profile, without any substance or reality. Rimbaud would understand. So . . . . *(drifts off).* It's what I've been telling you— everything is so goddamned controlled and orderly that you can't feel anything. Your senses are atrophied, no experience of excitement, of reality. It's all the same problem. Civilization destroys the real meaning of things.

GAF: I don't think that's sufficient to explain your feelings.

Jim: What do you mean?

GAF: I don't think that civilization, or the law, or the rules of society have anything to do with what you're experiencing. I've seen people who feel the way you do, and they all attempt to figure out why. Each has some explanation, as you do. But it seems to be that each has feelings similar to you and to the character in Camus' novel, and those feelings. . . of existential despair, are not the result of social forces in my experience.

Jim: So what're you saying, that there's something wrong with me? *(Jim is alert in the face of my confrontation, but there is still a bland,*

227

intellectualized quality to his questioning of me).

GAF: I'm saying that we need to look inside you for the answers to your feeling of boredom and agitation.

Jim: Yeah? Interesting idea. How's that any different than what I've been doing? Living on the edge, experiencing everything, no limits? I'm trying to experience the inside. *(drifting off)*.

GAF: My impression is that you've been escaping from the feelings, not exploring them. Experiencing the outer world isn't the same as reflecting on the inner one. And as a good example, as I mentioned earlier, it would be helpful to know what you're feeling when just being quiet and alone. You said 'bored and unreal.' How is that for you? What's it like?

Jim: *(Jim looks at me and*

228

shrugs. For a moment there is a far away look, a sense of preoccupation quickly followed by a return to a matter-of-fact attitude. Jim has gone as far as he can today.) I don't know. It's just there. I've got another recording session today. Have to go . . . .

GAF: Okay.

Jim came close to touching the dread within. But he is caught in the dilemma of having defended against it by rationalizing it as a by-product of society's conventions and therefore something to be "broken through" rather than resolved by self-reflection. He returns for the next session on time. He is subdued and non-combative and non-responsive. The likely explanation is that he felt some part of the dead zone and some sense of being understood, which both attracts and repels him at the same time.

Session 6.

Jim: *(Again he's dressed in black as seems to befit his mood. Avoiding eye contact, perhaps to avoid being upset like the last time, he slowly sits down, blanking starring at me, saying nothing).*

GAF: How are things?

Jim: Fine.

GAF: Have you had any thoughts about our last session?

Jim: No.

GAF: Mmm. I'm surprised at that. We seemed to have found some common ground. I wonder how you felt when you left?

Jim: Fine.

GAF: Mmm, well I ask because it seemed to me that we were beginning to sort some things out and that at the end of the session you felt better understood. Is that correct, or did I misread you?

Jim: Yeah, it was okay. So . . . now what? What am I supposed to do now? What difference does it all make? *(Jim is calm and detached. Part of him has withdrawn from the threat of being*

230

understood as he was in the previous session, while another part of him desperately wants to connect..)

GAF: Well, that depends on what you want. If you're interested in working on the nothingness and the alienation . . . if you don't want to feel like Camus' stranger, then there are some things we can do. But it'll take time and work.

Jim: *(Looks down and away as if considering my comments.)* How do we do that? Don't tell me this is all about Freud and the Oedipus complex.

GAF: Not quite. It's not about the Oedipus complex. *(In fact, Jim would be better off if it were. But his difficulties are based on disturbances that develop prior to the age at which Oedipal conflicts emerge).* Feelings of nothingness and unreality are

231

outcomes that tend to originate before Oedipal conflicts develop, around three to five.

Jim: Before? You mean before 3? (*Jim appears genuinely surprised.*)

GAF: Yes, but the glitch affects all subsequent developmental stages as well.

Jim: What can go wrong before the age of three? Christ!

GAF: We don't really know the cause, only the consequences.

Jim: (*Again looking off, out the window at trees bared of their leaves in the cold November light. He looks anguished to the depths of his being and one guesses that Jim is ever so lightly touching on his deepest despair.*) Look at that (*he points to the outside*). It's sterile—no life, no sensation, no existence.

Nothing tangible . . .
like me. *(almost to himself and sounding exhausted)*. Oh . . . God!

GAF: *(I can feel Jim's torment and I become more certain that he is living in the dead zone)*. You're living in dread of this nothingness, trying to find meaning in it. Perhaps it's time to contend with it.

Jim: Yeah? Maybe. How? If you're right and it started that fucking early, what can I do? What the fuck can I do? It's not like there's a drug I can take. I already do that. Even Freud can't fix this. *(Jim is verbally negative but hoping that he is wrong about Freud, and that I really can help him.)*

GAF: Well, the more we understand your experience the better we can help you organize it, reduce it, contain it, and then integrate it with the rest of your personality.

I know all these psychoanalytic ideas are complex and abstract. But they're powerfully explanatory. They enable us to help you work through your experience of nothingness and unreality.

Jim: Why nothingness? Why's everything unreal? *(Jim is very smart and thus having some way to comprehend his dilemma may be a critical need. Many patients do not want or need as much understanding as he might.)*

GAF: There are some excellent concepts that seem to account for these things. We can discuss them along the way if you wish. They wouldn't be very helpful to you right now.

Jim: Yeah? Well how much time will it take? *(Now*

Jim returns to a more guarded place— mistrust is a byproduct of living in the dead zone. There is neither relief nor a moment when the deadness isn't felt. In the face of that kind of immutability, who there could imagine trusting that it can change?)

GAF: That's uncertain. It's a very complicated problem and it may be several years.

Jim: Several years! Several years!

GAF: Well, you've lived with it all your life. It'll take a while to resolve it.

Jim: I don't get it yet. What happens before three? What could have happened to account for this? How do you know? *(His intelligence requires some cognitive grasp of the these possibilities. He again raises the question and grapples with it, a sign at times of hopefulness in the patient.)*

GAF: It's not easy to understand. We don't really know. There are many possibilities. The best clinical minds have attempted to explain, for example, your persistent conflict in relationships, your constant seeking of excitement, your tendency to withdraw, the contradictions, the impulsiveness, and the acting out behaviors as defenses against feelings of aloneness and high anxiety in infancy and early childhood—whatever the source of the anxiety. The nothingness, the sense of unrealness, and the despair can be seen as the result of the continued use of these defenses. To be sure, the defenses are very primitive. This is because they're developed early in life and never evolve into more advanced forms.

Jim: Defenses? How can feeling nothing and unreal be defenses? Didn't Freud . . . aren't defenses supposed to help? *(Again, Jim's intellect is at work here. He's asking rather sophisticated questions.)*

GAF: Yes, but the feelings of nothingness and unreality are not the defenses. They're the by-product of the only defenses available at those ages, that is— agitation, fantasy-formation, withdrawal from attachment, motoric action, and the separation of all experiences into good and bad feelings and images. And there is a mental process called splitting. Using the only defenses available to an infant and not having them evolve as the child grows can result in the feelings of dread, despair, emotional unevenness, and a special kind of inner aloneness.

Jim: Yeah? So you think you have the answers to this shit? How can you be sure? What evidence do you have? *(Jim is intrigued by the discussion, but his fundamental reason for asking these questions is, again, to elicit some possibility of hope.)*

GAF: Jim, the questions you ask have been and continue to be addressed in the clinical literature. I wonder if . . . if you're having difficulty holding back your doubt and mistrust because following rules and, uh . . .customs or the social conventions have never relieved those feelings of dread and agitation.

Jim: *(Jim is reflecting on my comments and stares off again.)* Nothing changes the way it is, or relieves it. Of course I doubt it. My experiences have taught me . . . that there's no means of escape from

238

the numbing of . . .
civilization. You argue
from . . . within that
perspective. You're
without experience in
my world of expanded
awareness . . . and
without the openness to
consider it. You're
smarter than I first gave
you credit for. You've
made a few good
points, but I can't see
that you're going to
make any real
difference. *(Jim is
scared and confused,
but he cannot let
himself trust or hope
because he has a low
tolerance for
disappointment or
frustration. It is
threatening to him and
so he cannot risk it—
another by-product of
the dead zone. Yet he is
desperate about his
inner chaos and he is
now challenging me to
convince him there is
hope.)*

GAF: You're right, I haven't
experienced the
nothingness and the
unreality that you talk

about. But I am familiar with those experiences clinically. In fact, almost everyone has had a few seconds, here and there, when a sense of nothingness and unreality happen. But it's too fleeting to cause the trouble you're having. And frankly, I doubt that assigning the blame for your feelings to civilization will help. It really hasn't helped, has it?

Jim: *(Smiling wryly. He is taking the challenge well, but he cannot accept my comments without diminishing them somehow.)* You have Freud's work to help support your position, and that's cool. But Freud knew that people were all fucked up by the rules and the bullshit, by the civilization's contradictions. How can you ignore that part of Freud? You must have read Norman Brown.

GAF: I hope we find that your

take on the cause of
your struggle is wrong.

Jim: What? Why?

GAF: Well, if civilization is
the problem, it's
difficult to see how
civilization can change
enough in our lifetime
to help with the despair
you feel. *(I'm falling
down here. It will not
help Jim if I am drawn
into a theoretical
discussion. What he is
again asking indirectly,
is, "can you really
help?")*

Jim: Yeah? What if you're
right?

GAF: I don't see the problem
that way. It seems that
what we need is a way
of understanding what
you're experiencing and
some way of working
through the despair.

Jim: Yeah. I don't know.
Maybe. What do we
do?

GAF: Next time we meet I'll
outline the way to

proceed, if you choose
to continue.

Jim: Yeah, okay.

Jim has come around a bit and we might be able to initiate psychotherapy. It remains to be seen whether he will really invest in the work. His need-fear dilemma is apparent. He desperately seeks relief from the constant emotional tumult, yet feels threatened by any chance of a connection to others. He will be unwavering in his detachment. His next appointment is canceled by his office. He shows up the following week for the eighth session. He has now come for two sessions more than required by the judge.

Session 8.

GAF: Good afternoon.

Jim: Hi.

GAF: Have you thought any further about the last session?

Jim: Yeah, some. Guess I'll see how it goes for a while.

GAF: *(This is the time to advise Jim on the basics for this form of therapy.)* Okay, let's discuss the way this form of therapy works and the basic requirements for it to work, to see if we can agree on a sort of compact. My responsibility will be to provide you with three weekly sessions at fixed times. The sessions will last fifty minutes. My commitment is to listen carefully and try to understand what you're experiencing. When I have an observation or comment to offer, I will. Your part will be to talk about yourself, your background, and current difficulties. If there are no specific problems at the time, then you should talk about any thoughts, feelings, behaviors, memories, dreams, and perceptions that come to mind. The more freely you communicate what's on your mind, the more we can learn, because in that way the significant conflicts and concerns usually surface. In a sense, it's the psychological equivalent of 'all roads lead to Rome.' Even if what passes through your mind at times seems inconsequential, it may assist us at some point if you verbalize it. My helpfulness to you depends on your efforts to make clear what you do know about yourself. At times, your thinking about these things will cause you to ask questions. I may not always answer, depending on my assessment of what would be most helpful to you at that time. Thus communications in therapy are a bit different than ordinary conversation. How does this description feel to you so far? *(This compact or explicit agreement on the specifics of the process is essential if we are to avoid the diversions and distractions that would be brought by the chaos of the borderline's inner world. The compact is to be used, in concert with psychoanalytic concepts regarding this complicated condition,*

*to stay on course and
keep the patient and
therapist focused on the
patient's internal state.
It also reassures the
patient about the
steadfastness of the
therapist and the
predictability of the
process. Thus, it goes a
long way toward giving
the patient the only
sense of object
constancy he may have
ever experienced).*

Jim: Yeah. Okay. What
       about gigs and tours out
       of state?

GAF: Well, those things can't
       be helped. We'll have
       to work around them as
       best we can.

Jim: And I have a problem
       with several years. I
       don't know where I'll
       be in a year.

GAF: Yes, those are concerns
       but we'll have to deal
       with them one at a time,
       if you decide to
       proceed. It's very
       important that we both
       understand and agree on

the framework for this form of therapy. Do you have any other questions or comments?

Jim: No, that's cool. But I still don't see where this is going.

GAF: We'll have to let it unfold, create a narration, a construction of sorts that clarifies and reveals. *(I'm being deliberately abstract here, yet Jim may be intrigued.)*

Jim: All right, how do we begin? *(Slouched comfortably in his chair)*

GAF: So you find the framework acceptable? No concerns?

Jim: Yeah . . . .

GAF: Well, we've already begun in a way. Talk about whatever comes to mind, as you have been doing.

Jim: But I'm still not sure

about you.

GAF: How do you mean?

Jim: You seem too formal, stiff . . . too rigid.

GAF: How does that cause you difficulty?

Jim: I can't talk to a stiff. You won't get it.

GAF: Won't get it?

Jim: Yeah.

GAF: I'm not following you.

Jim: Your obsolete thinking and ideas will get in the way of understanding what I'm saying.

GAF: You mean I can't allow for your points of view because my training and experience are—

Jim: You may want to understand but you really can't. Maybe you could get just a little of it, but not most of what my experience is all about.

GAF: By holding to my narrow views means I can't connect with your experiences in anyway useful to you?

Jim: You have your ideas and they might be useful to some.

GAF: In what way?

Jim: I couldn't guess. *(Jim is now back to oppositional, mistrustful behavior— as I expected he would be).*

GAF: So you'd really be wasting your time because my thinking is obsolete?

Jim: Yeah . . . it . . . it's uh, possible you have something of a spirit, a feeling for more than this. *(indicating the office and the 'civilized' world. Another part of Jim is hoping he's wrong and that I can get it and help him.)* But you're limited by your obsolete thinking.

GAF: So your sense of me is that I can't be of help to you because I don't have the right perspective. How would you feel different if I had the right one?

Jim: Maybe I could see some point to continuing this.

GAF: You've changed your mind then?

Jim: Changed my mind?

GAF: Yes. In our last session you seemed to think that we might do some exploring together. Now you're saying you don't think we can. How do you account for the change? (*Jim experienced me as positive and helpful in the last session, but it appears he now experiences me as useless: an ever shifting dichotomy of polarized characteristics, in this instance helpful-useless. So I am clarifying and confronting this shift in his internal*

249

experiences. These shifts in his attitude toward the external world are a constant source of confusion and disruption in his personal relationships.)

Jim: Well, I . . . *(He shrugs and turns away, a look of sadness on his face.)*

GAF: You know, I have a sense of something from you that I'll pass on if you wish.

Jim: Yeah?

GAF: I noticed during each of the sessions, that you seem to be on guard, apparently scrutinizing me, without revealing very much in the way of facial expression. You're very controlled. Sometimes you appear detached, as if you feel antagonistic, skeptical that I might be, uh, an adversary in some way, and that you need to remain cool and defiant.

Jim: Yeah . . . probably.

GAF: As if I were an inquisitor.

Jim: *(He shrugs again.)*

GAF: So perhaps your change of attitude is connected with this other view you have of me as a kind of antagonist, an enemy, and you resist reasoning that I have anything to offer you after all.

Jim: Yeah? Maybe. So what?

GAF: So . . . maybe you're expecting also that I have the same feeling of hopelessness that you do. Surely I couldn't help you in that case. On the other hand, you have engaged in discussion with me, have heard some of my thoughts. You've also showed up for two more sessions than required, and agreed to the idea of exploring your life further with me via the framework we discussed last time.

Jim: So what? (*Eyebrows raised and lips curled*

up on one side.)

GAF: Well, it may be that you're contending with powerful, malevolent internal demons that cause you to experience me as an antagonist who's powerless because of the very fact that I'm trying to help. And you then begin to think of me as being antagonistic toward you while believing you to be hopeless.

Jim: That's really stretching . . . .

GAF: Perhaps my observation is off the mark.

Jim: I didn't say you were antagonistic.

GAF: Mmm. Someone to be opposed?

Jim: No, not necessarily. I don't think your conclusions are valid. *(Jim withdraws into a long silence.)*

GAF: You appear to be reflecting on something.

252

Remember how this therapy works. You should relate what's on your mind to me in as unconstrained a manner as you can. Are you unable to talk about it?

Jim: No. I just want to know what's next.

GAF: I've reviewed with you how we must proceed. We're supposed to be exploring whatever's on your mind.

Jim: But I still don't feel that you can understand.

GAF: So my observation didn't help you to see how it is that you experience me that way?

Jim: I guess not.

GAF Well then, what do you think?

Jim: *(Stares off for a while.)* I don't know . . . I don't feel anything about it one way or the other.

GAF: But the result is you're

not going to engage the process of therapy—not going to talk?

Jim: I guess not.

GAF: Something in you is telling you to keep quiet?

Jim: Yeah, I suppose.

GAF: Your reluctance to speak and acknowledging that seems to validate my observation, wouldn't you say?

Jim: What do you mean?

GAF: You see in me something you're unable to see in yourself—antagonism and hopelessness. Yet it's the malevolent element within you that's in charge, urging you to be uncooperative with the process. To be uninvested, bland, cool. Don't trust . . . keep him on the hook.

Jim: Why should I if I don't think you or anyone can help?

254

GAF: That would seem to be specious reasoning. If you believe nothing and no one can help, why not just give up and end it. Your intelligence is being used here to support the malevolent elements within.

Jim: Yeah . . . .

GAF: Hmm. We seem to have come upon a critical piece of your conflict— the siren call of relief, coming from a part of you that urges you to resist, to oppose, and, if necessary, die. We've found the enemy and he is you. You might even attempt suicide tonight to underscore your resistance and hopelessness.

Jim: Yeah . . . so what?

GAF: You make my case.

Jim: Huh?

GAF: You're destroying the therapy by remaining silent and by wasting

255

our time together, in
part because you see me
as antagonistic and
unable to help.

Jim: *(Silence. The session
        ends.)*

By carefully examining the nature of the interaction in the
session, I am trying to make the point that what happens in the
therapy hour is as significant as what happens outside. During
this last session, I was attempting to clarify the hidden forces of
his inner world which he projects onto me. I therefore offer him
the emotional tone of the hour, point out the roles he has created
for me and himself, and identify the play he is enacting with me
as revealing how he externalizes a part of the dramatic conflict
going on in his internal, psychological world.

   Jim arrives for his next session still in his doubting
mood but slightly more active.

Session 9.

Jim: What do we do today?

GAF: Talk about whatever
        comes to mind.

Jim: Yeah, what difference
        does it make to you? I
        mean, you sound pretty
        sure of yourself. What
        makes you interested in
        doing this?

GAF: I'm interested, but
        you'll just have to
        accept that up front.

256

The real question is how we can overcome the part of you that will readily sabotage our work together. *(This problem of self-sabotage will remain throughout the whole of the therapeutic process.)*

Jim: Why bother then, if that's the case?

GAF: Well, there's another side of you that wants to work, wants to live and get healthier. You've returned, you're asking questions, and haven't acted to do harm to yourself—as if one part of you is hopeful and votes yes for living and the other is hopeless and votes no. The latter part can't stop thinking of me as hopeless and as a threat even as we talk.

Jim: Maybe. I still don't think you can understand.

GAF: Again, your saying that reflects one of the ways

you use your intelligence to rationalize, end treatment, and eventually your life.

Jim: Yeah . . . . Well, what now?

GAF: What comes to mind? As we discussed. *(Repetition is to be constant.)*

Jim: *(Silence. Jim looks calmly and blankly at me.)* Not much.

GAF: That's unlikely. It's hard to avoid having something on one's mind for very long. I also get the impression that you remain cynical about our work from the hint of a smirk on your face. So I must assume that you do not take our agreement very seriously and you're not saying what's on your mind. If so, we have to examine the reasons for your silence. One possible reason for your hesitancy is that you feel apprehensive or fearful of revealing yourself. But you don't appear as though you're fearful. Another possibility, based on our previous discussion, is that once again you're kept in a stalemate by the internal conflict between the part of you that seeks relief and the other part that seeks death. The healthy side is what gets you to the therapy sessions and on time, though it's no longer required. Yet the other side seems determined to frustrate us, and I see your passivity and silence as your giving in to that part.

Jim: What of it. What can be done?

GAF: What do you want to do?

Jim: So you're going to play Freud and not answer any questions? I ask and you won't answer?

GAF: Well, let me remind you

of the way this therapy works.

Jim: So I can't ask questions. You and Freud dictate. *(Defiantly looking around my office, Jim has noticed the psychoanalytic literature on my shelves and, of course, will use it to justify continuing his conflict with the therapy and himself.)*

GAF: You may ask. I'll answer some and not others, as I outlined to you in earlier sessions.

Jim: But I'm asking you a direct question. Are you going to simply ignore it, and act as though you didn't hear it? Is that what you call therapeutic? Or are you just mimicking Freud like a good little disciple?

GAF: Okay. Perhaps I should help you recall our earlier discussion about the way we must agree to work in this form of therapy. It requires that

260

you say whatever comes to mind without filtering it and that I offer my thoughts when they seem worthwhile. If your thoughts sometimes result in a question, I may answer or I may not, depending on my judgment as to whether a response might benefit you.

Jim: So, if you feel like it, right? Rather capricious of you, isn't it?

GAF: No, I'll respond if I feel it's helpful to you.

Jim: Yeah. So, Dr. Freud, you want to know about my life, all the gory details? *(Jim is not really giving up, but rather is just taking a new approach, although the part of him that seeks health is also present at the very moment that he is being difficult.)* You want to know about my friends?

GAF: Friends?

Jim: Yeah, like Pam, or Ray and Bobby and John?

GAF: Pam, Ray, Bobby, John?

Jim: Pam, my girl. She's cool. We fight . . . and make up. Ray, Bobby and John—my friends. You know I met Janis Joplin a while ago. She was a tough chick. It's too bad . . . about her death, I mean. We met at a party. She's a crazy bitch, whacked me in the head with a bottle. But I still think she was terrific.

GAF: You and Pam live together?

Jim: Yeah, couple of years now. (*Again slouched in his chair.*)

GAF: How is that relationship going?

Jim: You know. It's a relationship, uhh, with no rules, no restrictions. But she's my girl.

GAF: No restrictions?

Jim: Right. We do what feels good. We're not bound by the limits most people put on each other in relationships. I won't be bound by a straight jacket even if it comes in the form of society's mores. Even if it's accepted by everybody else.

GAF: *(I have a choice here: to address the effect of no rules on the relationship with Pam, or ask for clarification on how he is feeling when he has a need to engage in the extra-relationship activities.)* Do you find that when it's just you and Pam alone for a long time that you get antsy? That you feel the urge to go out and get action, an urge that's separate from your ideas about society's rules?

Jim: Huh . . . no. I see myself as an adventurer, an explorer. I seek meaning . . . meaning. Not walls, not bullshit.

(Jim is speaking, calmly, confidently, but I interpret his response here as a denial of his real inner agitation.)

GAF: So when you go out to seek adventure, you're engaged in an intellectual and sensory exploration?

Jim: Yeah, that's right. You're thinking that my exploring is really something else?

GAF: Well, I wonder. From a psychoanalytic point of view, of course . . . I wonder if your need for action in this way has other, unconscious motives.

Jim: Yeah? Like what?

GAF: Relief? Distraction? Protection?

Jim: What are you talking about? *(Jim has forgotten our discussion about how he constantly experiences despair.)*

GAF: How is it for you not to

264

go out, to stay with Pam instead?

Jim: It's fine sometimes. But it can get boring. I need to try everything, experience everything. Can't you . . . you must have a dull life if you don't get it, what I'm talking about.

GAF: Boring. You've used that word a lot. *(Boredom is a word used frequently by those in the dead zone when they try to identify their feelings of emptiness.)*

Jim: So? That's the way it is. With dulled senses and no way to bypass society's agenda, everything is boring.

GAF: Boring. Are there other feelings associated with it?

Jim: I don't know. *(irritated)* Who cares? What's the matter with you? I'll bet you were a four-eyed twit, teacher's pet, scared of girls and a bore as a kid. What was

265

your class standing? Bottom quarter, right? How can you do this for a living? Can't you get a real job? *(My question may have raised disturbing feelings in Jim, that is, put him in touch with the dread of the dead zone.)*

GAF: *(Brief silence as I let him stay with his hostility a bit.)* You found my question annoying. But our agreement was to explore the nature and meaning of your feelings, ideas, perceptions, behaviors, dreams. Remember?

Jim: Yeah, but that question's stupid. I don't know what you're talking about.

GAF: Mmm. Your angry reaction suggests to me that you do know. If I'm right, we should look to understand why you became so angry and avoided my question.

Jim: *(Silence)* We're

finished for today? Isn't
time up?

GAF: Yes, see you next time.

Jim: Yeah . . . maybe.

Once again Jim's behavior in this session reveals the difficulty
in treating this kind of patient, who often cannot recognize or
acknowledge the forces that drive him. Touching on the dead
zone illicits feelings of chaos and despair, thus Jim attacked me
when I pointed that out to him. He seeks relief from these
feelings through the use of the defenses of intellectualization,
avoidance, and the projection of his malicious dark side onto
others. He is truly a man in a titanic struggle for his soul, for his
own psychological existence.

Session 10.

Jim returns for a tenth session.

Jim: I'm going on my last
        tour next week so I
        won't be here.

GAF: Uh huh. When will you
        return?

Jim: In about eleven days.

GAF: Is it your intention to
        continue here?

Jim: Maybe. I guess so. I'll
        see when I get back.

GAF: Well, we'll have to

come to an agreement about your absences. The noncommittal way that you're leaving therapy reduces our chances of successfully treating you and doesn't square with your agreement to operate according to the framework we've agreed on. If you feel you're unable to meet your part of the agreement, then we should terminate our work until you feel more ready. *(I am giving Jim reassurance that I will not allow him to undermine the therapy by acquiescing to the forces in him which seek to defeat it .)*

Jim: What, are you kidding? Trying to be a hardass huh? So you won't let me decide when I get back?

GAF: You've already decided. That is, the part of you that kept you coming after your probation was up and the part of you that asked questions and searched for meaning—that part of you did decide. And now, once again, the self-destructive part is here, blocking your momentum toward health by being purposely vague about continuing.

Jim: Jesus! You're blowing this thing up. I have to go on tour. Is that so hard for your little mind to follow? What the fuck do you want—a guarantee written in blood? (*I am not being difficult. Jim can only benefit from this work if he can find a predictability in the therapy and in me. And the framework for the process and his collaboration within that framework can provide the anchor, the constant reference point for a man who has so little—almost no identity, tenuous attachments to others, and numbing pain about himself and his*

269

life.)

GAF: No, I'm simply reminding you that this therapy cannot work unless both of us adhere to the compact. You'll have to trust my judgment on this point.

Jim: All right, all right. I'll be here for the next appointment after I return. Satisfied? You're making a federal case out of a simple tour. What're you going to do when I leave for France in a few months? My last concert's in December, the twelfth I think, and then I'm finished with it all. Out!

GAF: That'll be your decision. I can arrange for you to see someone there, but it'll depend on your readiness to continue.

Jim: Yeah. Well I'm going. I'm a poet, that's what I was meant to be. I had a reading of my poetry last week. I didn't have

time to mention it last
time because you were
busy detailing the
therapy. Poetry's my
thing, man, and I intend
to be what I should
have been all along, a
poet. *(Long silence)*
Pam's back. She fucked
that imbecile Count she
knew from Paris. *(Jim
appears sad here for
just a moment.)* She
found me with Patricia.
*(Pat Kennealy, an
enigmatic, self
proclaimed witch, who
Jim married in an
occult ceremony while
wearing a black robe,
mixing blood, etc. It
isn't certain what Jim
thought of this
marriage.)* She found us
bare-assed on the floor .
. . She'll get over it.
*(Pam Courson had just
returned from Paris.
From what I could tell,
she was the only
constant figure in a life
consumed by turmoil.
This may be part of his
reason for returning to
her again and again
despite their fights and
his philosophy of no*

rules.)

GAF: *(Silence)*

Jim: Do you read anything but this stuff *(pointing to the books around my office)*, like poetry? Are you familiar with the Greek and Roman mythologies—Dionysus, Apollo? *(Jim looks at me expectantly and after a few moments glares at me).* What, asking intelligent questions offends your sensibilities? So you're not going to answer any questions?

GAF: As we agreed . . . when I feel it might be useful. *(Before responding to Jim's question I want to see where it's going in order to avoid intellectualizing the therapy.)*

Jim: Yeah, you're a victim of your training all right—a robot. You can't break loose from the fucking limitations of the world you live in. You claim to

272

understand more, but you don't. You expect me to fit neatly into your sterile, meaningless reality. Forget it. (_Jim is still standing, flipping through the pages of the book he has taken._)

GAF: Our agreement was that the purpose of this work was to help you to explore and sort out your situation. Any discussion of who I am and where I come from doesn't contribute to that purpose. We have repeatedly agreed on this point. Yet I can see that you persist in avoiding the agreed-upon, free-flowing narration of your thoughts and feelings. So I can only assume that the 'hellbent on destruction' part of you is in charge right now, that you're working toward becoming Nietzsche's 'philosopher of the dangerous,', and that martyrdom is your inevitable destiny. The

part of you that's
driving in this direction
is relentlessly opposed
to your work here. It
cloaks itself in
Nietzsche's philosophy
of the Antichrist, the
chaos of Rimbaud, and
the darkness of Kafka.
But behind all these
ideas are the driving
forces of self-hate and
an intolerable
emptiness. These forces
are sending you—
hurtling you to your
death. And the mystical
perspectives serve to
hide the truth from you.
*(I am addressing Jim's
inner world in the way
that I believe he
experiences it.)*

Jim: *(Just stares at me. He is
considering my
comments. After a few
minutes, he responds in
a less offensive voice.)*
So you . . . you have the
answers? You and
Sigmund? *(Jim's
sarcasm, though not
biting, clouds his
awareness of the
despair he feels. There
is a long silence)*. You

want me to talk? Want to know what's in my mind huh? I've already told you. Maybe you missed it, Gerald. It's about experience . . . it's Dionysian, taking a full measure of everything, spirit and flesh. No restrictions on our natural instincts. We've been here before, and I'm getting bored. (*Pauses, looks off vacantly*) Can't you dig it, man? Neitzsche's Antichrist, he's . . . totally, totally his own man, totally alone—the defiant one. (*Another long pause. Jim is meandering, his verbalizations are a mixture of free associations and fantasies.*) I'm like the shaman, touching the forces and power of other worlds, other . . . existences. (*Another lapse into a reflective silence. After a while, Jim looks up, and for a fleeting moment, flashes a look of unutterable agony. Then nothing. I take note of an instantaneous shudder passing through me, and remain silent. He then rambles on, staring blankly out the window).* You see, all the groundless worrying about good and evil, right and wrong, they just prevent the us from . . .uh . . . being in the true reality. The Antichrist defeats the true evil, the evil of nothingness, the dark nothingness of this reality. The meaningless nothingness. *(Another long pause and again the trance-like appearance.)* I once wrote a poem about . . . uh . . . it was called 'Horse Latitudes.' The Old World Spaniards sailing to the new world, would sometimes find themselves stuck in a static atmospheric condition—the doldrums . . . so they would lighten the ship by heaving the cargo over the side. Horses were often the main cargo. I could see them pushing these animals into the sea. Imagine them falling through the air and then struggling to stay afloat. But as their strength gave out, they would sink into the depths, sink . . . ever so slowly into the nothingness of the sea.(*Another brief silence, and then he continues.*) So you see, the only solution is to destroy the illusion of this fake reality, to break through to the other reality. Do you see, man, it's all fake . . . all fake. *(Jim turns and looks at some books in a bookcase next to his chair, gets up and scans one title, then another and another until he has read the titles of a dozen or more. He is drawn to A Psychoanalytic Study Of The Myth of Dionysus And Apollo_by Helene Deutsch and Object Love And Reality: An Introduction To A*

Psychoanalytic Theory Of Object Relations by Arnold Modell.) Are these some of your sacred texts, your guides to reality? Who is Helene Deutsch? *(Opening the book cover he reads the subtitle).* "Two variants on the son-mother relationship. The son who saves, the son who kills." What's this bullshit? Who is this chick? If this is what you're reading . . . what a bummer. Is she talking about Dionysus and Apollo in terms of their mothers? Christ, everything with Freud is mother. He was a genius but he had a one track mind. Dionysian mythology had it right on. The only way out of the meaninglessness of his existence . . . the senses, and raw, unfettered experience. And what are object relations? This guy Modell . . . does he mean people? Why doesn't he say so? What reality does he mean?

You still have nothing to say? *(Jim is still standing, trying to engage me in an intellectual discussion.)*

GAF: Well, I can see how you would be attracted to both Dionysus and Neitzsche's Antichrist-Redeemer. I've been noticing again how you continue to talk about meaninglessness and nothingness.

Jim: Yeah . . . you're on that road again. Why Dionysus?*(Jim is somewhat curious despite his cynicism. He also has hidden hopes that I have a solution for his despair.)*

GAF: Live life to the fullest, gratify the senses, experience everything, and maybe the meaninglessness will become meaningfulness, the nothingness may then become something.

Jim: Yeah, yeah I know. And the Antichrist . . . uh . . .

that's where my self-destructive side shows up. *(Jim is sarcastic but he is talking about his beliefs and he is still harboring some hope of rescue from the Dead Zone.)*

GAF: Yes, the Antichrist is one of the ways the malevolent forces within you are pulling you toward death. They say, 'accept the chaos, revel in the darkness, embrace death since you cannot escape the nothingness.'

Jim is trying to reject my comments but they touch on what he is experiencing and he becomes stuck. His internal momentum to self-destruct is just slowed by the realization that my observations are speaking to his true feelings and dilemmas. He stares out the window again, appearing to drift into a kind of calm, emotional place. He is in a state similar to a toddler playing in the same room as mom, not interacting with her, but doing his own thing. This state of emotional well being while in the "present-non-interacting-acting other" has been described by the British Analyst W. W. Winnicott as the capacity to be alone, alone together, and is a significant step in a child's development.

The session ends after more discussion of arrangements for future meetings. This session has further revealed the persistent threat to the life preserving instincts found in the dead zone.

Jim will come for fourteen more sessions before leaving the Doors and moving to France. The next session is the last one. He is leaving for France in four days.

Session 24.

Jim: *(As expected he is better and worse).* Well, maybe you've made a few points, Gerald. You're not so bad for who you are. But I'll be glad to get out of here.

GAF: Uh huh. Do you want the names of a few therapists in Paris?

Jim: Yeah, sure. If it makes you feel better. Can't you let it alone? I'm going to be working on my poetry. I'll see what happens. *(Despite his attitude, Jim sounds less certain and even worried. He sits down, his anger not in evidence.)*

GAF: You're vague and noncommittal about this, and I fear that if you don't continue your work with an experienced therapist, you will not do well in Paris.

Jim: Well, your pessimism is encouraging. My life isn't dependent on therapy, or on you, or on anyone. You keep making the same point over and over. Why won't I do well? ? *(Jim's voice still sounds more anxious than angry.)*

GAF: What has changed? You still feel the same confusion about who you are, the same nameless dread that causes you to act self destructively. The same impulses toward chaos and death. What makes you believe that these forces of despair won't be with you wherever you go?

Jim: Because I have my poetry. That's who I am and it's enough. And Paris is the place. *(Sensing that I'm skeptical of his plan, Jim sits forward, obviously angry.)* What? What? You're pissing me off. Can't you dig it? I'm not like everybody else. Don't measure me by the norms you use for others. I've been different from the beginning.

GAF: Perhaps. But what reason can there be for you to reject the idea of continuing with a therapist except to block your progress toward emotional health?

Jim: Maybe I don't need this bullshit. Maybe I think you're a fucking asshole and I'm wasting my time.

GAF: *(Sitting back in his chair, Jim looks miffed becoming silent. Jim is desperately trying to maintain his emotional distance. He is doing that now by rejecting me and devaluing the work we have done together.)* Mmm. Perhaps you need to be angry with me and to dismiss the work we've done.

Jim: Oh yeah? Why?

GAF: Because you might be feeling sad at leaving. And anger is easier, a shield against the feeling.

Jim: (*Faint smile, looking away.*) Yeah, sure. Why would I miss this—and having to pay for it, too.

GAF: Because it may be the first time you have felt hope, and found some relief for your confusion and angst. And maybe because you think of me as a friend you'll be leaving.

Jim: (*Silence. I have touched on Jim's inner experience at this moment and he is now feeling the sadness. But historically he has shown little tolerance for this place in the human heart, and he will soon leave it and me behind as with all his close relationships. For a moment I think I see his eyes become moist, but quickly*

284

passes.)

Jim: Yeah . . . yeah. Just give
me the fucking names if
it makes you happy. I
told you, you're okay.
Maybe you have some
interesting   ideas.
Maybe I'll look up one
of these geniuses. (*I
hand him a slip with the
names   of   several
Parisian   analysts.*)
Thanks.

Jim Morrison died in Paris of an apparent overdose of heroin.
We cannot be certain that his descent into the "knowing void"
could have been halted, that a continuation of the psychotherapy
constructed in this book would have saved him. The scope of the
tragedy of his early death is widened when one considers that he
did not understand the nature of the forces arrayed against him.
While he sensed that something was wrong, he was unable to
comprehend what it was.

Epilogue

This book has been written for all of those who suffer the torment of life in the dead zone. We hope we have provided our readers with a very different understanding of the lives of Janis Joplin and Jim Morrison. We have shown how inaccurate were the many popular explanations of how each died, and how inadequate were the descriptive accounts of their everyday struggles. While we have nothing but superlatives for their biographies and biographers—undertaken with great care as they were by noted authors—we have nonetheless revealed how each external account of the two performers was not able to place the disparate details of their lives into a coherent, causal explanation. As described earlier, the developments in clinical research during the twenty-five years since Janis and Jim died have provided us with a very useful framework within which to explain the personality disorders that took their lives.

We think, however, that our analysis here may offer readers more than a very revealing answer to the question, "What was wrong with them?" The insights into the lives of Janis and Jim that we have provided are, we think, interesting enough, especially to those who retain a strong interest in their music and personalities. But we believe these insights have broader applications to many, many others in our society who suffer from the various types of borderline disorders. So, in a sense, our account of two borderline personalities may assist not only other clinicians and psychotherapists to recognize patients so afflicted, but might also help to establish a line between the social and the psychological, between the easy acceptance of individual idiosyncracies and the common recognition of emotional imbalance.

Our work here may thus help a larger audience—one less familiar with the complications of personality disorders—to distinguish merely eccentric, flashy, and indecent behaviors from those behaviors that are suggestive of serious emotional illness. As we cast our gaze backward onto the tumultuous decade of the 1960s, we cannot but notice the then prevailing popular tendencies to legitimate the odd and bizarre, the "hyper" and the "hipper," the excessive and obsessive. We heard the disciples of Timothy Leary urging us to tune out and turn on, to "do your own thing," to join the revolution and "seize the time." It is not our intention to quarrel with those who espoused such messages, nor to demonize them. Rather we chose to disclose the relationship that existed between the very popular socio-political thematics that characterized the 60s, widely embraced as they were by those who idolized Janis and Jim, and the easy acceptance of the self-destructive behaviors for which Janis and Jim were so well known.

To frame this differently, to a significant extent, the many outrageous behaviors exhibited by Janis and Jim were legitimated by a thin veneer of respectability that was supported by those sympathetic to countercultural expressions prevalent during the 60s. Making this claim does not undercut the role that other forces and factors may have played in the adulation of behaviors that proved so lethal to Janis and Jim.

So, for example, that they were two very talented, highly artistic and very successful performers and musicians also helped to deflect substantial criticisms of their "antics" on stage, which were as likely to be confused with sophisticated artistic merit as they might have been associated with emotional disturbance. That many fans often associated the two with "anti-establishment" political positions, with a profound recognition of the alienative affects of post-industrial capitalism, with the consequences of an unpopular and ill-fated Southeast Asian war, could understandably have deflected anyone from noticing what we might easily observe today to be severe emotional distress. Clinical research was not yet ready to identify and treat the symptoms of their emotional conflicts and dread, while the great socio-political turmoil of the decade had many mesmerized by the power and energy of their performances. Thus, Janis and Jim performed themselves to death, embraced by their awe-struck fans who were already inclined to see only the mystical, the raucous, and the dazzle.

Of course, this work has had the benefit of retrospect, of a more informed backward glance at the 60's through the prism of modern psychiatry and psychology. So we hope this work will help our readers disentangle the forces in play that led to the tragic deaths of Janis and Jim.

Appendix I

DSM-IV Criteria For Borderline Personality Disorder--

A pervasive pattern of instability of interpersonal relationships, self-image, and affects, and marked impulsivity beginning by early adulthood and present in a variety of contexts, as indicated by five (or more) of the following

1. frantic efforts to avoid real or imagined abandonment.
Note: Does not include suicidal or self-mutilating behavior covered in Criterion 5.

2. a pattern of unstable and intense interpersonal relationships characterized by alternating between extremes of idealization and devaluation.

3. identity disturbance: markedly and persistently unstable self-image or sense of self.

4. impulsivity in at least two areas that are potentially self-damaging (e.g., spending, sex, substance abuse, reckless driving, binge eating).
Note: Does not include suicidal or self-mutilating behavior covered in Criterion 5.

5. recurrent suicidal behavior, or threats, or self-mutilating behavior.

6. affective instability due to a marked reactivity of mood (e.g., intense episodic dysphoria, irritability, or anxiety usually lasting a few hours and only rarely more than a few days.

7. chronic feelings of emptiness.

8. Inappropriate intense anger or difficulty controlling anger (e.g., frequent displays of temper, constant anger, recurrent physical fights).

9. transient, stress-related paranoid ideation or severe dissociative symptoms.

*Published By The American Psychiatric Association

Appendix II

DSM-IV Criteria for Major Depressive Episode

A. Five (or more) of the following symptoms have been present during the same 2-week period and represent a change from previous functioning; at least one of the symptoms is either (1) depressed mood or (2) loss of interest or pleasure.
Note: Do not include symptoms that are clearly due to a general medical condition, or mood-incongruent delusions or hallucinations.

1. depressed mood most of the day, nearly every day, as indicated by either subjective report (e.g., feels sad or empty) or observation made by others (e.g., appears tearful).
Note: In children and adolescents, can be irritable mood.

2. markedly diminished interest or pleasure in all, or almost all, activities most of the day, nearly every day (as indicated by either subjective account or observation made by others)

3. significant weight loss when not dieting or weight gain (e.g., a change of more than 5% of body weight in a month), or decrease or increase in appetite nearly every day. Note: In children, consider failure to make expected weight gains.

4. insomnia or hypersomnia nearly every day.

5. psychomotor agitation or retardation nearly every day (observable by others, not merely subjective feelings of restlessness or being slowed down).

6. fatigue or loss of energy nearly every day

7. feelings of worthlessness or excessive or inappropriate guilt

(which may be delusional) nearly every day (not merely self-reproach or guilt about being sick).

8. diminished ability to think or concentrate, or indecisiveness, nearly every day (either by subjective account or as observed by others).

9. recurrent thoughts of death (not just fear of dying), recurrent suicidal ideation without a specific plan, or a suicide attempt or a specific plan for committing suicide.

*Published By The American Psychiatric Association

Bibliography

<u>Clinical Literature</u>

Deutsch H: "Some Forms of Emotional Disturbance and Their Relationship to Schizophrenia." *Psychoanalytic Quarterly*, 11:301-321.

Diagnostic and Statistical Manual of Mental Disorders (fourth edition). Washington: The American Psychiatric Association, 1994 [DSM IV]

Grinker, R. R., Sr., Werble, B., & Drye, R. C. (1968), *The Borderline Syndrome*. New York: Basic Books.

Grotstein, J. S., Solomon, M. F. & Lang, J. A. (1987) *The Borderline Patient: Emerging Concepts in Diagnosis, Psychodynamics, and Treatment*. Vols. I & II, Hillsdale, New Jersey: Analytic Press.

Gunderson J. (1977) *"Characteristics of Borderlines."* In *Borderline PersonalityDisorders*, ed. P. Hartocollis. New York: International Universities Press, pp. 173-192.

Gunderson, J. (1982), "Empirical Studies of the Borderline Diagnosis." In *Psychiatry,* 1982: Annual Review, ed. L. Grinspoon. Amer. Psychiat. Press, pp. 415-436.

Gunderson, J. & Kolb, J. (1978), "Discriminating Features of Borderline Patients." *Amer. J. Psychiat.*, 135(7):792-796.

Gunderson, J. & Singer, M. T. (1975) "Defining Borderline Patients: An Overview." *American Journal of Psychiatry*, 132:1-10.

Kernberg O. (1967) "Borderline Personality Organization."

Journal of the American Psychoanalysis Association 15:641-685.

Kernberg O. (1976) "Technical Considerations in the Treatment of Borderline Personality Organization." *Journal of the American Psychoanalysis Assoc*iation 24:795-829.

Kernberg O. (1975) *Borderline Conditions and Pathological Narcissism*. New York: Jason Aronson.

Kernberg O. (1984) *Severe Personality Disorders*: Psychotherapeutic Strategies. New Haven: Yale University Press.

Meissner, W. (1984) *The Borderline Sprectrum*. New York: Jason Aronson.

Perry, J. C., & Klerman, G. L. (1978) "The Borderline Patient." *Archives of General. Psychiatry.*, 35:141-150.

Winnicott D W: (1965) *The Maturational Processes and the Facilitating Environment*. New York: International Universities Press.

Janis Joplin

Amburn, E. (1992) *Pearl: The Obsessions and Passions of Janis Joplin*. New York: Warner Books.

Caserta, Peggy. (1973) *Going Down With Janis,* as told to Don Knapp. New York:Dell

Freidman, Myra. (1992) *Buried Alive*. New York: Harmony Books

Joplin, Laura. (1992) *Love, Janis*. New York: Villard Books

Film: *Janis, The Way She Was*. (1974 documentary), MCA
 Home Video 80080.

Jim Morrison

Densmore, John. (1990) *Riders on the Storm*. New York:
 Delacorte Press.

Hopkins, Jerry & Sugarman, Danny. (1980) *No One Here Gets
 Out Alive*. New York: Warner Books.

Kennealy, Patricia. (1992) *Strange Days: My Life With and
 Without Jim Morrison*. New York: Dutton.

Morrison, Jim. (1970) *The Lords and the New Creatures*. New
 York: Simon & Schuster.

---------- (1988) *Wilderness*. New York: Villard Books

---------- (1990) *The American Night*. New York: Villard Books.

Riordan, James & Prochnicky, Jerry. (1991) *Break on Through:
 The Life and Death of Jim Morrison*. New York: William
 Morrow.

About the Authors

Gerald A. Faris, Ph.D. is a clinical psychologist with more than 20 years of hospital inpatient, private practice and supervisory experience. He received his doctorate from The Graduate Faculty of the New School for Social Research in New York and was a Clinical Instructor in Psychiatry at the Yale University School of Medicine. Dr. Faris has drawn on his extensive clinical experience in presenting Janis and Jim as the extraordinarily talented, intelligent and tormented individuals they were.

Ralph M. Faris, Ph.D. has presented the sociological commentary and analysis of the era in which Janis and Jim lived. He is a professor of sociology and the director of the Honors Program at the Community College of Philadelphia, where he has recently won the National Lindback Foundation, Distinguished Teaching Award.

To Scott + Mons
good friends

Jerry Jas

Living in the Dead Zone:
Janis Joplin and Jim Morrison

To greater understanding.

Rafh m Farr

Living in the Dead Zone:
Janis Joplin and Jim Morrison

by

Gerald A. Faris and Ralph M. Faris

ISBN 1-58500-185-6

About the Book

The Faris' have written a modern clinical analysis, detailing a surprising coincidence about the lives of Janis Joplin and Jim Morrison. They raise and answer the following questions: **Why did they behave so outrageously? Why were they so self-destructive? What did they have in common? What could have helped them? What really killed them?**

Their work examines how Janis Joplin and Jim Morrison, the 'king and queen' of rock and roll, suffered from a little understood psychiatric disorder that eventually took their lives. To form the conclusions in their book, they carefully analyze the voluminous literature, films and other pertinent information about the two performing artists. At the same time, they develop the imaginary but revealing psychotherapy sessions with Janis and Jim. They have constructed the therapy sessions in a way that is both entertaining and sympathetic to help clarify the nature and complexity of this disorder. They provide those curious about Janis and Jim with a very provocative, plausible and dramatic account of their lives.

Their analysis is based on the close scrutiny of secondary works pertaining to the two, on the biographies, films and magazines that sought to characterize their lives and deaths. Of course, they had no direct opportunity to interview them, nor to provide them with therapy. In that sense, the therapy sessions are a kind of faux activity. But they have studied everything that was ever written about Janis and Jim and have developed an analysis that is highly probable and cogent. If their analysis is correct, and if we knew then what we know now about the disorder that took their lives, then the therapy sessions developed in their book are as close as possible to what they might have been, had they actually sought help from a psychoanalytically trained clinician.

You may, however, find it difficult to categorize this book. It isn't a psychohistory of the two performers in the conventional sense of the genre, nor is it based on actual therapeutic encounters with them and of course it isn't a typical psychobiography. Nothing comparable exists in the literature. Focusing on the lives and deaths of these two controversial characters, the Faris' convincingly describe how their outrageous behaviors and self-destructive impulses were part of a complex and confusing condition known to clinicians as a "borderline personality disorder." Through the intense, poignant, hypothetical psychotherapy sessions with each of them, the authors reveal the devastating and relentless nature of this disorder. The book is clinical in theme, lyrical and narrative in style and deeply sympathetic to the real suffering of Janis and Jim. This analysis differs from previously published materials that *described* their outrageous behaviors, temperaments, moods and personalities, in that it provides an *explanation* for the behaviors that led to their premature deaths.

The psychotherapy sessions are perhaps the most captivating aspect of the book. By letting Janis and Jim "speak" through these sessions, the Faris' provide surprising insights about their outrageous behaviors and emotional turmoil. The drama and intensity of these exchanges between Janis and Jim and a modern, experienced clinician/therapist will captivate as much as they inform.